The Comprehensive Guide to
WOODWORKING

Practical Plans, Step-by-Step
Instructions,Techniques, Advanced
Tips and Tools for Crafting Perfect
Wood Projects

GABRIEL ANDREWS

CONTENTS

INTRODUCTION

Woodworking is a craft that has been around for centuries. It is the art of creating functional and beautiful objects out of wood using simple tools and techniques. From furniture to decorative pieces, woodworking has been an integral part of human history and culture. It is a hobby that can be enjoyed by anyone, regardless of age, gender, or skill level. Whether you are an experienced woodworker or just starting out, **The Comprehensive Guide to Woodworking** is the perfect book for you.

This all-inclusive guide covers everything you need to know about woodworking, from the basics of selecting wood and using hand tools to advanced techniques for crafting intricate designs. The book is filled with practical plans, step-by-step instructions, and tips that will help you create stunning wood projects that you can be proud of.

The book highlights an overview of the different types of wood and their characteristics. You will learn how to select the right wood for your project, how to measure and cut wood accurately, and how to prepare it for use. It also teaches basic woodworking techniques, such as sawing, drilling, and sanding. These techniques are essential for any woodworker, and the book provides clear instructions to help you master them.

Once you have mastered the basics, the book then guides you through more advanced woodworking techniques, such as joinery, veneering, and carving. These techniques require more skill and precision, but with the help of the book, you will be able to create beautiful and complex wood designs.

The Comprehensive Guide to Woodworking also includes a section on tools and equipment. You will learn about the different types of hand tools and power tools that are essential for woodworking, as well as how to use them safely and effectively. The book also provides tips on how to maintain and care for your tools, so that they last for years to come.

In addition to the practical aspects of woodworking, the book also covers design principles and aesthetics. You will learn how to create designs that are both functional and visually appealing, and how to use color, texture, and grain to enhance the beauty of your wood projects.

The book is written in a clear and concise style, with step-by-step instructions. Whether you are a beginner or an experienced woodworker, you will find something useful in this guide. The book also includes a range of projects, from simple birdhouses to complex cabinets, so that you can put your new woodworking skills to the test.

Woodworking is a rewarding and fulfilling hobby that can provide a sense of accomplishment and satisfaction. With The Comprehensive Guide to Woodworking, you will have all the tools and knowledge you need to create beautiful and functional wood projects that you can be proud of. Whether you are looking to start a new hobby, improve your skills, or create a special gift for someone, this book is the perfect resource for all your woodworking needs.

CHAPTER 1

WHAT IS WOODWORKING?

Woodworking is the art and craft of creating objects from wood using various tools and techniques. It involves designing, cutting, shaping, joining, and finishing wood to create functional or decorative objects such as furniture, cabinets, sculptures, and musical instruments.

The history of woodworking can be traced back to ancient times when humans first learned to use tools to shape wood for various purposes. Over the years, woodworking has evolved from a basic craft to a sophisticated industry with advanced technologies and techniques.

Woodworking involves a wide range of tools and techniques, including hand tools such as saws, chisels, planes, and hammers, as well as power tools such as drills, sanders, routers, and saws. These tools are used to shape, cut, and join wood into the desired form.

In addition to tools, woodworking also requires an understanding of wood itself. Different types of wood have unique characteristics that affect their strength, flexibility, and appearance. Woodworkers must know how to choose the right wood for their project and how to work with it effectively.

One of the most important aspects of woodworking is joinery, which refers to the method used to connect two or more pieces of wood together. There are many types of joinery techniques, including dovetail joints, mortise and tenon joints, and butt joints, among others. Each technique has its strengths and weaknesses, and choosing the right one depends on the project at hand.

Finishing is another essential aspect of woodworking. It involves applying a coating or finish to protect the wood from moisture, wear, and tear, and to enhance its appearance. Finishes can be natural or synthetic, and they can be applied using various techniques, including brushing, spraying, and wiping.

Woodworking is a versatile and rewarding hobby or profession that requires skill, creativity, and patience. It allows woodworkers to express their creativity and to create functional and beautiful objects that can last for generations. Whether you are a beginner or an experienced woodworker, the possibilities are endless, and the satisfaction of creating something with your own hands is immeasurable.

Types of Woodworking Projects

Woodworking is an age-old craft that has been practiced for thousands of years. It involves creating objects and structures from wood, using a variety of tools and techniques. Woodworking projects can range from small, simple items like picture frames and cutting boards to large-scale constructions like buildings and furniture. In this article, we will explore the different types of woodworking projects, from beginner-level to advanced.

Small Projects:

Small woodworking projects are perfect for beginners who are just starting to learn the craft. These projects typically require minimal tools and materials, making them affordable and easy to complete. Examples of small projects include:

a) Cutting boards - A cutting board is a great first project because it only requires a few tools and a piece of wood.

It can be made from any type of wood and can be customized to fit any kitchen.

b) Picture frames - Picture frames are another beginner project that can be completed with just a few tools. They can be made from a variety of woods and can be customized to fit any photo.

c) Jewelry boxes - Jewelry boxes are a bit more advanced than cutting boards and picture frames, but they are still a great beginner project. They require a few more tools and a bit more time, but the end result is a beautiful and functional piece of furniture.

Furniture Projects:

Furniture projects are more complex than small projects and require a greater degree of skill and tools. These projects typically involve building larger structures such as chairs, tables, and cabinets. Examples of furniture projects include:

a) Tables - Tables come in a variety of shapes and sizes, from coffee tables to dining tables. They require a variety of tools and materials, but the end result is a beautiful and functional piece of furniture.

b) Chairs - Chairs are another furniture project that can be customized to fit any style or space. They require a variety of tools and materials, including upholstery, but the end result is a beautiful and functional piece of furniture.

c) Cabinets - Cabinets are a bit more complex than tables and chairs, but they are still a popular furniture project. They require a variety of tools and materials, including hardware, but the end result is a beautiful and functional piece of furniture.

Home Improvement Projects:

Home improvement projects involve using woodworking skills to improve the appearance and functionality of a home. These projects can range from building a deck to installing new kitchen cabinets. Examples of home improvement projects include:

a) Deck building - Building a deck is a popular home improvement project that requires a variety of woodworking skills. It involves designing and building a structure that is both beautiful and functional.

b) Kitchen remodeling - Kitchen remodeling involves building and installing new cabinets, countertops, and other features. It requires a variety of woodworking skills and can greatly improve the appearance and functionality of a home.

c) Built-in furniture - Built-in furniture is a great way to maximize space and improve the functionality of a home. It involves building furniture that is built into the walls or other structures of a home.

Artistic Projects:

Artistic woodworking projects involve using woodworking skills to create beautiful and unique works of art. These projects can range from sculptures to intricate carvings. Examples of artistic woodworking projects include:

a) Sculptures - Sculptures are a popular woodworking project that require a high degree of skill and creativity. They can be made from a variety of woods and can be customized to fit any style or space.

b) Carvings - Carvings are another artistic woodworking project that require a high degree of skill and creativity. They can be made from a variety of woods and can be customized to fit any style or space.

c) Woodturning - Woodturning is a form of woodworking that involves using a lathe to shape and carve wood. It is a popular artistic woodworking project that can be used to create a variety of objects such as bowls, vases, and other decorative items.

Advanced Projects:

Advanced woodworking projects are for those with a high degree of skill and experience in the craft. These projects require a variety of tools and techniques, and often involve complex designs and structures. Examples of advanced woodworking projects include:

a) Musical instruments - Building a musical instrument requires a high degree of skill and knowledge of woodworking techniques. It involves using a variety of tools and materials to create a functional and beautiful instrument.

b) Wooden boats - Building a wooden boat is a complex and time-consuming project that requires a variety of woodworking skills. It involves building a hull, deck, and other structures using a variety of techniques and materials.

c) Timber framing - Timber framing involves building structures using large, heavy timber beams and posts. It requires a high degree of skill and knowledge of woodworking techniques, and often involves complex designs and structures.

As shown in this section, woodworking projects can range from small and simple items to complex and advanced structures. Whether you are a beginner or an experienced woodworker, there is a woodworking project that can challenge and inspire you. With the right tools, materials, and techniques, you can create beautiful and functional objects that will last for generations.

Woodworking Tools and Materials

Woodworking tools and materials are essential to the success of any woodworking project, and it's important to choose the right ones for the job. In line with the preceding statement, we will discuss woodworking tools and materials in detail, including their uses, benefits, and types.

Woodworking Tools

1. Hand Tools:

Hand tools are used for the shaping and finishing of wood. These tools include chisels, saws, hammers, planes, screwdrivers, and many others. They are primarily used for precision work and are useful for small projects or when working with delicate materials.

2. Power Tools:

Power tools are used for larger and more complex projects. They are powered by electricity or compressed air and include drills, sanders, saws, routers, and many others. Power tools are faster and more efficient than hand tools, making them ideal for larger woodworking projects.

3. Measuring and Marking Tools:

Measuring and marking tools are used to ensure accuracy and precision in woodworking. These tools include measuring tapes, squares, calipers, and marking knives. They are essential for ensuring that pieces of wood are cut to the correct size and shape.

4. Safety Gear:

Safety gear is essential when working with woodworking tools. This includes safety glasses, gloves, and hearing protection. Woodworking can be dangerous, and it's important to protect yourself while working.

Woodworking Materials

a. Lumber:

Lumber is the primary material used in woodworking. It is typically made from hardwoods or softwoods and comes in a variety of sizes and shapes. Lumber is used for a variety of projects, including furniture, cabinetry, and flooring.

b. Plywood:

Plywood is made by gluing together thin sheets of wood. It is a versatile material that is used for a variety of woodworking projects, including cabinetry and furniture.

c. Veneer:

Veneer is a thin layer of wood that is applied to the surface of another material. It is used to give the appearance of solid wood without the expense. Veneer is often used in furniture making.

d. Finishing Materials:

Finishing materials are used to protect and enhance the appearance of wood. This includes stains, varnishes, and oils. These materials can be used to give wood a specific color or finish, and can also protect it from damage.

Choosing the Right Tools and Materials

Choosing the right tools and materials for a woodworking project is essential for its success. It's important to consider the type of project, the materials being used, and the level of experience of the woodworker. For example, a beginner woodworker may prefer hand tools over power tools, while a more experienced woodworker may prefer the speed and efficiency of power tools.

In sum, woodworking tools and materials are essential to the success of any woodworking project. Hand tools, power tools, measuring and marking tools, and safety gear are all important for precision and accuracy. Lumber, plywood, veneer, and finishing materials are used to create beautiful and functional pieces of furniture and cabinetry. When choosing tools and materials, it's necessary to consider the type of project and the level of experience of the woodworker. With the right tools and materials, anyone can create beautiful and functional woodworking projects.

A drill in use

CHAPTER 2

BASIC WOODWORKING SKILLS

Woodworking is a remarkable art that allows you to create stunning furniture, decorative pieces, and other objects using the natural beauty of wood. Whether you're new to the craft or an experienced woodworker, mastering the basic woodworking skills is the first step towards creating truly remarkable work that will amaze and inspire others.

At the core of woodworking is a deep appreciation for the craftsmanship that goes into creating beautiful and functional objects. To succeed in this craft, it's essential to develop a deep understanding of the foundational skills that form the backbone of woodworking.

The first step in achieving mastery of woodworking is to prioritize safety. By taking the necessary precautions to protect yourself and others, you can work with confidence and peace of mind. Keeping your workspace clean and organized and ensuring that your workpiece is securely in place is essential for creating a safe and efficient work environment.

Accurate measuring and marking are crucial for achieving precision and consistency in woodworking projects. With the right tools and a steady hand, you can create precise cuts and angles that will bring your vision to life.

Cutting is an integral part of woodworking, and mastering different cutting techniques such as crosscutting, ripping, and mitering is essential for creating high-quality work. With practice, you can hone your skills and develop the ability to create intricate and beautiful pieces that will delight and inspire.

Joinery is the process of connecting two pieces of wood to create a sturdy and durable joint. By learning to master various types of joinery, you can create works of art that will stand the test of time and inspire admiration for generations to come.

Sanding is a critical step in the woodworking process that requires patience and attention to detail. By using the right sandpaper grit and taking the time to sand the wood evenly and thoroughly, you can create a smooth and flawless surface that will provide the perfect foundation for your finishing techniques.

Finishing is the final step in the woodworking process and allows you to showcase your creative vision by enhancing the natural beauty of the wood. With a variety of techniques to choose from, such as staining, painting, and varnishing, you can bring your work to life and create a piece that is truly unique and inspiring.

Mastering basic woodworking skills is a journey that requires patience, dedication, and a deep love for the craft. By prioritizing safety, developing a deep understanding of the foundational skills, and honing your craft over time, you can create stunning works of art that will inspire and delight others for years to come. So go forth, embrace the craft, and let your creativity run wild!

Types of Joints

As a woodworking expert, understanding the different types of joints is crucial to creating a sturdy and beautiful piece of furniture or other woodworking project. Joints are the way in which two or more pieces of wood are joined together, and there are a variety of different joint types that are used for different purposes.

Butt Joint

The simplest type of joint is the butt joint, which is created by simply butting two pieces of wood together at right angles. This type of joint is often used for simple projects, but it is not particularly strong, and is more prone to splitting than other types of joints.

Lap Joint

The lap joint is another simple joint that is created by overlapping two pieces of wood and then fastening them together with nails or screws. This type of joint is stronger than a butt joint, but it is still not ideal for heavy-duty applications.

Mortise and Tenon Joint

The mortise and tenon joint is one of the strongest and most traditional types of joints used in woodworking. It is created by cutting a rectangular hole (the mortise) in one piece of wood, and then inserting a matching rectangular peg (the tenon) from the other piece of wood into the hole. This type of joint is very strong and is commonly used in furniture making.

Dovetail Joint

The dovetail joint is another traditional joint that is often used in furniture making. It is created by cutting a series of interlocking shapes (usually in the form of a series of trapezoids) into the two pieces of wood that are being joined together. When the two pieces are assembled, the interlocking shapes create a very strong joint that is resistant to pulling apart.

Tongue and Groove Joint

The tongue and groove joint is a type of joint that is commonly used for flooring and paneling. It is created by cutting a slot (the groove) into one piece of wood and a matching protrusion (the tongue) into the other piece of wood. When the two pieces are joined together, the tongue fits snugly into the groove, creating a strong and stable joint.

Miter Joint

The miter joint is created by cutting two pieces of wood at a 45-degree angle and then joining them together to form a right angle. This type of joint is often used for picture frames and other decorative projects, but it is not particularly strong and is prone to splitting.

Biscuit Joint

The biscuit joint is created by cutting a slot into two pieces of wood and then inserting a thin, oval-shaped piece of wood (known as a biscuit) into the slot. The two pieces of wood are then glued together, and the biscuit helps to align the pieces and add extra strength to the joint.

Understanding these different types of joints is essential for any woodworking project. By choosing the right joint for the job, you can ensure that your finished product is strong, durable, and beautiful.

Measuring and Marking

Measuring and marking are essential skills in woodworking. Accurate measurements and markings are necessary for ensuring that pieces fit together correctly and for achieving the desired aesthetic results. In this section, we will discuss the tools and techniques used for measuring and marking in woodworking.

Tools for Measuring and Marking

There are several tools that woodworkers use for measuring and marking, including:

1. Tape Measures: Tape measures are used for measuring long distances accurately. They come in various lengths, typically ranging from 6 to 35 feet. Some tape measures have a locking mechanism that keeps the tape in place when measuring.

2. Rulers: Rulers are used for measuring shorter distances, typically up to 12 inches. They come in various sizes, including both metric and imperial units.

3. Squares: Squares are used for marking and checking 90-degree angles. There are several types of squares, including try squares, framing squares, and speed squares.

4. Compasses: Compasses are used for marking circles and arcs. They consist of two arms that can be adjusted to different distances apart.

5. Marking Gauges: Marking gauges are used for marking parallel lines and measuring distances from an edge. They consist of a beam with a sliding fence that can be locked in place at a desired distance.

6. Combination Squares: Combination squares are a versatile tool that combines the features of a ruler, square, and protractor. They can be used for marking and

checking angles, measuring distances, and checking the flatness of a surface.

7. Bevel Gauges: Bevel gauges are used for measuring and transferring angles. They consist of a handle and a blade that can be adjusted to a desired angle.

Techniques for Measuring and Marking

Accurate measurements and markings are critical to the success of any woodworking project. Here are some techniques for ensuring accurate measurements and markings:

a. Use the Right Tool: Use the appropriate tool for the job. For example, use a ruler for short measurements and a tape measure for longer ones.

b. Measure Twice, Cut Once: This age-old adage reminds us to check our measurements before making any cuts. Double-checking measurements can save a lot of time and material in the long run.

c. Use Sharp Tools: Sharp tools are essential for making accurate markings. Dull tools can create inaccurate lines, which can throw off the entire project.

d. Make Clear, Consistent Marks: Use a pencil or marking knife to make clear, consistent marks. Faint or inconsistent markings can cause confusion and errors.

e. Use Reference Lines: Use reference lines to ensure that measurements and markings are consistent and accurate. For example, use a square to mark a line perpendicular to an edge.

f. Measure From the Same Reference Face: When marking multiple pieces that need to fit together, measure from the same reference face to ensure that they are all the same size.

e. Take Into Account the Kerf: When making cuts, take into account the width of the saw blade. This is known as the kerf, and failing to account for it can result in pieces that do not fit together correctly.

Please note that measuring and marking are essential skills in woodworking. Accurate measurements and markings are necessary for ensuring that pieces fit together correctly and for achieving the desired aesthetic results. By using the right tools and techniques, woodworkers can ensure that their projects are successful and enjoyable to create.

Cutting

Cutting is one of the most important skills in woodworking, and it is essential for creating precise and accurate pieces of furniture or other wooden objects. Cutting involves using a variety of tools to remove material from a piece of wood in order to shape it or join it with other pieces of wood. There are several different types of cutting techniques and tools that are commonly used in woodworking, and mastering these techniques is crucial for any serious woodworker.

One of the most basic cutting techniques in woodworking is sawing. There are several different types of saws that are commonly used in woodworking, including hand saws, table saws, and circular saws. Hand saws are the most basic type of saw and are used for cutting pieces of wood by hand. Table saws and circular saws are more advanced types of saws that are used for cutting larger pieces of wood or for making precise cuts.

Another important cutting technique in woodworking is planing. Planing involves using a hand plane or power planer to remove material from the surface of a piece of wood. This technique is used to create flat surfaces or to remove imperfections from the surface of a piece of wood.

Planing is also used to create joints, such as mortise and tenon joints, which require precise cuts to fit together properly.

Chiseling is another essential cutting technique in woodworking. Chisels are used to remove material from the surface of a piece of wood by chipping away at it with a sharp edge. Chiseling is commonly used to create intricate designs or to remove material in tight spaces where other tools cannot be used.

Another crucial cutting method in woodworking is drilling. Drills are used to create holes in pieces of wood, which can be used for a variety of purposes, such as creating joints or attaching hardware to a piece of furniture. There are several different types of drills that are commonly used in woodworking, including hand drills, power drills, and drill presses.

Finally, routing is another important cutting technique in woodworking. Routers are used to remove material from the edge of a piece of wood by using a spinning cutting bit. Routing is commonly used to create decorative edges or to create grooves in a piece of wood for attaching hardware or other pieces.

In addition to these cutting techniques, there are several different types of cutting tools that are commonly used in woodworking. These tools include hand saws, power saws, chisels, planes, drills, and routers, as well as a variety of other specialized cutting tools that are used for specific tasks.

Mastering the art of cutting is essential for any serious woodworker, and it requires a combination of skill, patience, and practice. By understanding the different cutting techniques and tools that are commonly used in woodworking, and by practicing these techniques on a regular basis, any woodworker can become an expert in the art of cutting and create beautiful and precise pieces of furniture and other wooden objects.

Sanding, Shaping and Finishing

As a woodworker, achieving a smooth and polished finish on your projects is one of the most important and satisfying aspects of the craft. This is where sanding, shaping, and finishing come into play. In this chapter, we will explore these techniques in depth and provide you with the knowledge and skills you need to produce beautiful, high-quality woodworking projects.

Sanding

Sanding is a fundamental process in woodworking that involves removing the top layer of wood fibers using abrasive materials such as sandpaper. Sanding is essential for removing rough spots, scratches, and other imperfections from the surface of the wood. Sanding can also help you achieve a smooth and polished finish.

There are several types of sandpaper available, each with a different grit level. The grit level of sandpaper refers to the size of the abrasive particles on the paper. Sandpaper with a higher grit level has smaller abrasive particles and is used for fine sanding. Lower grit levels are used for removing rough spots and shaping the wood.

When sanding, it's important to keep the following tips in mind:

1. Always sand with the grain of the wood. Sanding against the grain can cause scratches and other imperfections.

2. Start with a coarse sandpaper and work your way up to a finer grit. This will help you achieve a smooth and polished finish.

3. Use a sanding block or a sanding machine to ensure an even sanding surface.

4. Wipe the surface of the wood with a damp cloth after sanding to remove any dust particles.

Shaping

Shaping is the process of creating specific shapes and curves in the wood. This is often done using a combination of hand tools and power tools such as routers and jigsaws. Shaping can be used to create decorative details or to fit a piece of wood into a specific space or shape.

There are several techniques and tools used in shaping, including:

Hand planes – Hand planes are used to remove thin layers of wood from the surface of the wood. They are essential for creating smooth and even surfaces.

Chisels – Chisels are used to remove small pieces of wood and create fine details.

Routers – Routers are used to create decorative details and shapes in the wood. They can be fitted with different bits to create different profiles and shapes.

Jigsaws – Jigsaws are used to cut curves and shapes in the wood. They can be fitted with different blades to create different cuts.

When shaping, it's important to keep the following tips in mind:

a. Always use sharp tools. Dull tools can cause the wood to splinter and produce rough cuts.

b. Take your time and work slowly. Rushing can lead to mistakes and uneven cuts.

c. Use clamps or a vise to hold the wood in place while you work. This will ensure that the wood remains stable and doesn't move while you're working on it.

Finishing

Finishing is the final step in the woodworking process. It involves applying a protective layer to the surface of the wood to protect it from moisture, dirt, and other elements. Finishing can also enhance the natural beauty of the wood and give it a polished and professional look.

There are several types of finishes available. These include:

1. Stains – Stains are used to change the color of the wood. They penetrate the surface of the wood and can be used to create a variety of colors and shades.

2. Sealers – Sealers are used to create a barrier between the wood and the environment. They protect the wood from moisture and other elements.

3. Varnishes – Varnishes are used to create a glossy and durable finish. They can be applied in several layers to create a high-quality finish.

4. Paints – Paints are used to completely cover the surface of the wood with a specific color. They can be used to create a variety of finishes, including glossy, matte, and textured finishes.

When choosing a finish, it's imperative to consider the type of wood you're working with, as well as the purpose of the finished product. Some finishes may work better with certain types of wood, while others may be more suitable for outdoor use or high-traffic areas.

When applying a finish, keep the following tips in mind:

- Always apply the finish in a well-ventilated area.

- Follow the manufacturer's instructions for application and drying times.

- Use a brush, roller, or sprayer to apply the finish evenly.

- Sand the surface of the wood between coats to ensure an even and smooth finish.

- Wipe the surface of the wood with a damp cloth after applying the finish to remove any dust particles.

- Allow the finish to dry completely before using or handling the finished product.

The treble techniques of sanding, shaping, and finishing are essential in woodworking and can help you achieve a beautiful and polished finish on your projects. By following these tips and using the right tools and materials, you can create high-quality woodworking projects that will stand the test of time. Remember to take your time, work carefully, and enjoy the process of creating something beautiful with your own hands.

Sanding a work

CHAPTER 3

WOODWORKING PLANS AND PROJECTS

Woodworking is an age-old craft that involves creating useful or decorative items from wood. From simple chairs and tables to complex cabinets and shelves, woodworking has been an integral part of human culture for centuries. Woodworking plans and projects are the blueprints and instructions that woodworkers use to create these items. In this overview, we'll explore the world of woodworking plans and projects and discuss the different types of plans, their benefits, and how to get started with woodworking.

Types of Woodworking Plans

Woodworking plans can be broadly classified into two categories: project plans and furniture plans.

Project plans are designs for smaller, standalone items that can be completed in a single day or weekend. These plans typically include detailed instructions, a list of required materials and tools, and a set of drawings or diagrams to guide the builder. Some common examples of project plans include birdhouses, jewelry boxes, picture frames, and cutting boards.

Furniture plans, on the other hand, are designs for larger, more complex items such as chairs, tables, and cabinets. These plans may require several days or even weeks to complete and often involve more advanced woodworking techniques. Furniture plans typically include detailed measurements, cutting diagrams, and step-by-step instructions for each stage of the building process.

Benefits of Woodworking Plans

Using woodworking plans can provide a number of benefits for woodworkers of all skill levels. Here are just a few of the advantages of working from plans:

1. Clear guidance: Woodworking plans provide clear instructions and diagrams, making it easier for woodworkers to understand how to build a project or piece of furniture.

2. Saves time: With a detailed plan in hand, woodworkers can save time by avoiding mistakes and working more efficiently.

3. Ensures accuracy: Plans often include precise measurements and cutting diagrams, ensuring that each component of a project or piece of furniture is cut to the correct size.

4. Allows for customization: While plans provide a blueprint for a project, they can also be modified and customized to suit the builder's preferences or needs.

Getting Started with Woodworking Plans

If you're new to woodworking, the prospect of working from plans may seem daunting. However, with a few basic tools and some patience, anyone can learn to build items from wood. Here are some tips to help you get started:

a. **Choose the right plan:** Select a plan that matches your skill level and interests. Starting with a simple project plan can help build confidence and skills before moving on to more complex furniture plans.

b. **Gather the right tools:** A few basic tools such as a saw, drill, and sandpaper are all that is needed to get started. As you progress, you can add more specialized tools to your collection.

c. **Practice safety:** Woodworking can be dangerous, so it's important to practice safety at all times. Always wear protective gear such as goggles and gloves, and use tools only as intended.

d. **Take your time:** Woodworking is a slow, deliberate process. Rushing through a project or piece of furniture can lead to mistakes and frustration.

In a nutshell, woodworking plans and projects offer a way for anyone to create beautiful and functional items from wood. With the right plan, tools, and approach, even beginners can learn to build birdhouses, cutting boards, and other simple projects. For more experienced woodworkers, furniture plans offer a challenge and a chance to hone their skills. Whether you're a beginner or an expert, woodworking plans and projects offer a satisfying and rewarding hobby that can last a lifetime.

Designing Plans and Projects

Woodworking is a skilled craft that requires a great deal of planning and preparation. To create high-quality and successful woodworking projects, it's crucial to have a clear plan in place. This plan should outline the entire project, from the initial design to the final touches. In this article, we'll explore the importance of designing plans and projects in woodworking, and provide practical examples of how to do so effectively.

Why is Designing Plans Important in Woodworking?

Designing plans is critical to the success of any woodworking project. It allows the woodworker to anticipate potential issues and address them before they become problems. A well-designed plan can help the woodworker to avoid costly mistakes, wasted time, and wasted materials. Additionally, a clear plan can help the woodworker to stay on track and complete the project efficiently.

Another crucial aspect of designing plans is that it allows the woodworker to envision the final product. By visualizing the finished product, the woodworker can make sure that they have all the necessary tools, materials, and skills to complete the project successfully. Moreover, a well-designed plan can help the woodworker to ensure that the final product meets their expectations.

Practical Examples of Designing Plans and Projects in Woodworking

1. Creating a Cutting List

One of the first steps in designing a woodworking project is to create a cutting list. A cutting list is a detailed list of all the pieces of wood required for the project. The list should include the type of wood, the dimensions of each piece, and the number of pieces required.

For example, if you were designing a simple wooden chair, your cutting list might include:

- Four legs, each measuring 2 inches by 2 inches by 18 inches

- Two side rails, each measuring 2 inches by 1 inch by 16 inches

- One back rail, measuring 2 inches by 1 inch by 20 inches

- Five slats, each measuring 2 inches by 1 inch by 14 inches

By creating a cutting list, you can ensure that you have all the necessary materials before starting the project. This will save you time and prevent you from having to make multiple trips to the hardware store.

2. Sketching the Project

Once you have your cutting list, the next step is to sketch the project. This involves creating a rough drawing of the finished product. Your sketch should include dimensions, angles, and any special features of the project.

For example, if you were designing a wooden bench with a curved backrest, your sketch might look something like this:

By sketching the project, you can visualize the final product and make any necessary adjustments before starting to cut the wood.

3. Creating a Detailed Plan

Once you have your cutting list and sketch, the next step is to create a detailed plan. This plan should include step-by-step instructions on how to build the project. It should also include a list of tools and materials required for each step.

For example, if you were designing a wooden bench, your plan might look something like this:

Step 1: Cut the legs to size using a table saw

Materials required: Four 2-inch by 2-inch by 18-inch pieces of wood

Tools required: Table saw, measuring tape

Step 2: Cut the side rails to size using a miter saw

Materials required: Two 2-inch by 1-inch by 16-inch pieces of wood

Tools required: Miter saw, measuring tape

Step 3: Assemble the frame using wood glue and clamps

Materials required: Legs, side rails, wood glue, clamps

Tools required: Clamps, wood glue

And so on.

By creating a detailed plan, you can stay organized and ensure that you don't miss any steps or materials. It also allows you to identify any potential challenges or obstacles that may arise during the project and come up with solutions before starting.

4. Mockup or Prototype

A mockup or prototype is a scaled-down version of the final product. It can be a useful tool to test and refine the design before starting the actual construction. Mockups can be made using cheap or scrap materials and can be easily modified if needed. They can help the woodworker to test different angles, shapes, and dimensions to make sure that the final product is functional and aesthetically pleasing.

For example, if you were designing a wooden desk, you could create a mockup using cardboard or foam board. This would allow you to test different heights, widths, and depths to find the perfect dimensions for the desk.

5. Using Software

With the advancements in technology, there are now many software programs available that can help woodworkers design and plan their projects. These programs allow the woodworker to create 3D models of their designs, test different materials and finishes, and create accurate cutting lists and plans.

For example, SketchUp is a popular 3D modeling software that is often used by woodworkers. It allows the user to create detailed models of their designs, test different materials and finishes, and create accurate plans and cutting lists. Other software programs that are commonly used by woodworkers include AutoCAD, Fusion 360, and SolidWorks.

Designing plans and projects in woodworking is essential for creating high-quality and successful projects. It allows the woodworker to anticipate potential issues, visualize the final product, and stay organized throughout the project. By following the practical examples outlined in this article, woodworkers can create detailed plans and cutting lists, sketch their projects, create detailed plans, make mockups or prototypes, and use software to design and plan their projects. With careful planning and preparation, woodworkers can create beautiful and functional pieces that they can be proud of.

Building and Measuring

Woodworking is a craft that has been around for thousands of years, and it's no secret why. The process of transforming raw pieces of wood into beautiful, functional objects is a satisfying and rewarding experience. One of the key components of successful woodworking is the ability to build and measure accurately. In this section, we will explore the importance of building and measuring in woodworking, and some tips and techniques to help you improve your skills.

Building in woodworking refers to the process of creating a project from raw pieces of wood. This can be as simple as building a small shelf, or as complex as building a piece of furniture with multiple pieces and joints. Regardless of the project, the ability to build accurately is crucial for a successful outcome. Inaccurate measurements can result in pieces that don't fit together properly, joints that are weak, or even an entire project that is unusable.

To build accurately, you must start with accurate measurements. There are many tools available to help you measure accurately, including rulers, tape measures, squares, and more. One of the most important aspects of accurate measuring is consistency. If you are using a ruler, for example, make sure you always measure from the same end. If you are using a tape measure, make sure you use the same side of the tape each time. These small details can make a big difference in the accuracy of your measurements.

In addition to using the right tools and being consistent, it's also important to understand the concept of "measure twice, cut once." This means that you should always double-check your measurements before making any cuts. It's much easier to fix a measurement error before making a cut than it is to try to fix it afterwards. Taking the time to double-check your measurements can save you a lot of time and frustration in the long run.

Another important aspect of building accurately is the ability to make precise cuts. This requires both the right tools and the right technique. For example, a table saw is an excellent tool for making straight cuts, but it's important to make sure the blade is aligned properly and that you use a guide to keep the wood straight as you cut. A bandsaw, on the other hand, is great for making curved cuts, but it's important to keep the blade tensioned properly and to use the right blade for the job.

Once you have your pieces cut accurately, the next step is to join them together. Joinery is a critical aspect of woodworking, as it is what holds your project together. There are many different types of joints as mentioned in chapter two, which included butt joints, lap joints, mortise and tenon joints, and more. Each type of joint has its own strengths and weaknesses, and the key is to choose the right joint for the job.

One practical example of building in woodworking is constructing a bookshelf. The first step in building a bookshelf is to decide on the type of wood to use. Different types of wood have different characteristics, such as hardness, density, and grain pattern. These characteristics will affect the overall appearance and durability of the bookshelf. Once the wood has been selected, the woodworker must cut the wood to the correct size and shape. This requires accurate measurement and precision cutting tools, such as a table saw or a miter saw.

After the wood has been cut, the woodworker must join the pieces together. There are several methods for joining wood, such as using nails, screws, dowels, or glue. The choice of joining method will depend on the design of the bookshelf and the type of wood being used. For example, if the bookshelf is designed to hold heavy books, screws or dowels may be a better choice than nails or glue. The woodworker must also ensure that the joints are strong and secure, as a weak joint can cause the bookshelf to collapse or warp over time.

When it comes to measuring for joinery, precision is even more important than for basic cuts. A joint that is even a fraction of an inch off can result in a weak or unstable joint. One technique that can help ensure accuracy is to use a marking gauge to mark the location of the joint. This can help ensure that you make your cuts in exactly the right place.

Measuring is not only important for building, but also for finishing your project. For example, if you are staining or painting your project, it's important to measure the amount of stain or paint you need and mix it in the correct proportions. If you are applying a finish, such as polyurethane, it's important to measure the amount of finish you need and apply it evenly.

In addition to measuring accurately, it's also important to measure consistently. For example, if you are staining a large project, make sure you use the same amount of stain for each section. If you are applying a finish, make sure you apply the same number of coats to each part of the project. Consistency in your measurements and application techniques will ensure a uniform and professional finish.

When it comes to measuring in woodworking, you should understand the properties of the wood you are working with. Wood is a natural material, and its properties can vary depending on the species, the age of the tree, and how it was cut. For example, a piece of wood that has been cut with the grain will be stronger and more stable than one that has been cut against the grain. Understanding the properties of the wood you are working with can help you make more informed decisions when it comes to measuring and cutting.

Also ensure you measure accurately, understanding the properties of the wood. There are, however, other techniques you can use to improve your building and measuring skills. One of these is to practice, practice, practice. The more you work with wood and the more projects you complete, the more confident and skilled you will become.

Another technique is to seek out advice and guidance from more experienced woodworkers. Joining a woodworking club or taking a class can be a great way to learn from others and improve your skills. You can also find a wealth of information online, including tutorials, forums, and videos that can help you learn new techniques and improve your skills.

Remember, building and measuring are critical components of successful woodworking. Accurate measurements are essential for creating pieces that fit together properly, while precise cuts and joinery are what hold your project together. By using the right tools, being consistent in your measurements, understanding the properties of the wood, and practicing your skills, you can improve your building and measuring skills and create beautiful, functional objects that you can be proud of. So go ahead, pick up your tools, and start building!

Troubleshooting In Advanced Woodworking

Advanced woodworking can be a fulfilling and rewarding activity, but it can also be frustrating when things don't go as planned. One of the most important skills to have when working with wood is troubleshooting, or the ability to identify and solve problems as they arise.

Now, let's discuss some common issues that woodworkers may encounter and offer tips on how to troubleshoot them.

Issue #1: Wood Warping

One of the most frustrating problems that woodworkers may encounter is wood warping. This occurs when the wood starts to bend or twist, making it difficult to work with. There are a few reasons why wood may warp, including:

- Uneven moisture: If one side of the wood is exposed to more moisture than the other, it can cause the wood to warp.

- Incorrect storage: If wood is stored improperly, it can warp over time.

- Incorrect milling: If the wood is not milled correctly, it can cause the wood to warp.

To troubleshoot this issue, try the following:

- Use a moisture meter to check the moisture content of the wood. If one side is significantly wetter than the other, flip the wood over and let it dry out evenly.

- Store wood in a dry, cool place with good ventilation.

- Make sure your wood is milled correctly before starting your project.

Issue #2: Splintering

Splintering occurs when the wood tears or breaks along the grain, leaving rough edges or sharp points. This can be a safety hazard and can also ruin the look of your project. Splintering can be caused by:

- Dull tools: If your tools are dull, they can cause the wood to splinter.

- Incorrect tool use: If you're using a tool incorrectly, it can cause splintering.

- Poor-quality wood: Low-quality wood may be more prone to splintering.

To troubleshoot this issue, try the following:

- Use sharp tools when working with wood.

- Take your time and use proper techniques when using tools.

- Choose high-quality wood for your projects.

Issue #3: Uneven Stain or Finish

Uneven staining or finishing can be frustrating because it can ruin the look of your project. This can be caused by a few different things, such as:

- Uneven sanding: If the wood is not sanded evenly, it can cause the stain or finish to be uneven.

- Inconsistent application: If the stain or finish is applied inconsistently, it can cause uneven coloring.

- Incorrect application: If the stain or finish is applied incorrectly, it can cause uneven coloring or streaks.

To troubleshoot this issue, try the following:

- Sand your wood evenly before staining or finishing.

- Take your time and apply your stain or finish carefully and consistently.

- Follow the manufacturer's instructions for applying the stain or finish.

Issue #4: Wood Cracking

Cracking can occur in wood when it dries out too quickly or is exposed to extreme temperatures. This can be frustrating because it can ruin the structural integrity of your project. Cracking can be caused by:

- Rapid drying: If wood dries out too quickly, it can cause cracking.

- Extreme temperatures: If wood is exposed to extreme heat or cold, it can cause cracking.

- Overexposure to sunlight: If wood is exposed to too much sunlight, it can cause cracking.

To troubleshoot this issue, try the following:

- Let your wood dry slowly and evenly.

- Store your wood in a dry, cool place with good ventilation.

- Avoid exposing your wood to extreme temperatures or direct sunlight for extended periods.

Issue #5: Joints Coming Apart

One of the most frustrating issues that woodworkers may encounter is joints coming apart. This can be caused by a few different things, some of which are:

- Poor joinery: If the joints are not made correctly, they may come apart over time.

- Incorrect glue application: If the glue is not applied correctly, it can cause joints to come apart.

- Wood movement: As wood expands and contracts with changes in temperature and humidity, it can cause joints to loosen.

To troubleshoot this issue, try the following:

- Make sure your joinery is made correctly and that all pieces fit together tightly.

- Use the appropriate type of glue for your project and follow the manufacturer's instructions for application.

- Allow sufficient time for the glue to dry and cure before putting pressure on the joint.

- Consider reinforcing the joint with additional hardware, such as screws or dowels.

- Allow for wood movement when designing and constructing your project.

Issue #6: Tearout

Tearout occurs when the wood fibers are torn out during cutting, leaving a rough or jagged edge. This can be caused by a few different things, including:

- Dull tools: If your tools are not sharp, they may tear out the wood fibers.

- Incorrect tool use: If you're using a tool incorrectly, it can cause tearout.

- Grain direction: Cutting against the grain can cause tearout.

To troubleshoot this issue, try the following:

- Use sharp tools when working with wood.

- Take your time and use proper techniques when using tools.

- Pay attention to the direction of the grain and adjust your cutting technique accordingly.

- Consider using a backer board or sacrificial piece of wood to prevent tearout.

Troubleshooting is an essential skill for any woodworker, especially those working on advanced projects. By identifying common issues and taking steps to prevent or address them, you can ensure that your woodworking projects are successful and satisfying. Remember to take your time, use proper techniques, and choose high-quality materials to achieve the best results. With practice and patience, you can become a skilled troubleshooter and tackle even the most challenging woodworking projects with confidence.

CHAPTER 4

FURNITURE PROJECTS

Furniture projects are a popular and rewarding aspect of woodworking. These projects involve creating functional and aesthetically pleasing pieces of furniture that can be used in homes, offices, or other settings. The range of furniture projects that can be undertaken is vast, from simple tables and chairs to complex cabinetry and decorative pieces.

Furniture projects require a variety of woodworking skills and techniques, including measuring and cutting wood, joining pieces together, sanding and finishing, and applying stains or paints. Some furniture projects may also require the use of specialized tools such as routers, table saws, or planers.

One of the key aspects of furniture projects is design. Woodworkers must consider factors such as the intended use of the furniture, the style and aesthetics of the piece, and the type of wood that will be used. They may create their own designs or follow plans provided by others.

There are many different types of furniture projects that woodworkers can undertake. Some popular examples include:

- **Tables:** Coffee tables, end tables, dining tables, and more.

- **Chairs:** Dining chairs, lounge chairs, rocking chairs, and more.

- **Cabinets:** Kitchen cabinets, bathroom cabinets, bookcases, and more.

- **Beds:** Platform beds, canopy beds, bunk beds, and more.

- **Decorative pieces:** Mirrors, picture frames, vases, and more.

Furniture projects can be undertaken by woodworkers of all skill levels, from beginners to experienced professionals. They offer a great opportunity to learn new skills, experiment with different design ideas, and create beautiful and functional pieces of furniture that can be enjoyed for years to come.

Coffee Tables

Designing and producing coffee tables is a challenging yet rewarding woodworking project. A coffee table is often the centerpiece of a living room, and a well-crafted piece can add both functionality and style to a space. In this guide, we'll explore some creative design ideas and production techniques to help you make a stunning coffee table that stands out from the rest.

Choose the right wood:

The first step in creating a beautiful coffee table is selecting the right wood. Choose wood that is both durable and attractive, such as oak, walnut, or cherry. These hardwoods have a natural beauty that will make your table stand out. Consider the color and grain pattern of the wood, as well as its hardness and resistance to wear and tear.

Choose the shape and size:

The shape and size of your coffee table will depend on your personal taste and the space available in your living room. Consider a round or oval shape for a more organic look, or a square or rectangular shape for a more traditional style. The height of the table should be comfortable for both sitting and standing, and the size should be appropriate for the space available.

Add unique features:

To make your coffee table truly stand out, consider adding unique features such as built-in storage, a glass top, or a live edge. Built-in storage can be in the form of drawers, shelves, or hidden compartments, providing a functional element to the table. A glass top can add a modern touch and showcase the beauty of the wood underneath. A live edge table, where the natural edge of the wood is preserved, can add a rustic or natural element to the design.

Use interesting joinery techniques:

The joinery technique you choose can also add interest and uniqueness to your coffee table. Consider using a dovetail joint, a mortise and tenon joint, or a biscuit joint to connect the pieces of wood. These joinery techniques not only add strength to the table but also showcase the craftsmanship of the woodworker.

Finish with care:

The finishing process is crucial in bringing out the beauty of the wood and protecting it from wear and tear.

Consider using a natural oil or wax finish to highlight the natural color and grain of the wood. A lacquer or polyurethane finish can add durability and protection from spills and scratches.

Experiment with color:

Wood can be stained or painted to add color and visual interest to your coffee table. Experiment with different stains or paint colors to achieve the desired effect. Consider adding a pop of color to a more neutral table, or using a subtle stain to highlight the grain pattern of the wood.

Use reclaimed wood:

Using reclaimed wood can add an interesting backstory and character to your coffee table. Look for wood that has a history, such as old barn wood or salvaged lumber. These materials can add a rustic or industrial element to your design.

In designing and producing a coffee table, you need to pay rapt attention to choosing the right wood, shape, and size, adding unique features, using interesting joinery techniques, finishing with care, experimenting with color, and using reclaimed wood, so you can create a one-of-akind masterpiece that reflects your personal style and craftsmanship.

Practical Plan for Producing a Coffee Table

Materials:

- 2 pieces of hardwood (oak, walnut, cherry, etc.) measuring 40" x 20" x 1"

- 4 pieces of hardwood measuring 16" x 1" x 1"

- 4 hairpin legs with screws

- Wood glue

- Sandpaper (120-grit and 220-grit)

- Natural oil finish

Tools:

- Table saw

- Miter saw

- Router

- Drill

- Clamps

- Orbital sander

Steps:

1. Cut the two pieces of hardwood to 40" x 20" using a table saw.

2. Cut the four pieces of hardwood to 16" using a miter saw.

3. Use a router to create a 1/4" wide by 1/2" deep groove in each of the 40" sides of the tabletop pieces. This will be where the 16" pieces will fit into.

4. Use wood glue to attach the 16" pieces into the grooves of the tabletop pieces, forming a rectangular box.

5. Clamp the pieces together and let them dry overnight.

6. Sand the coffee table with 120-grit sandpaper to remove any rough spots and splinters.

7. Sand the coffee table again with 220-grit sandpaper to create a smooth surface.

8. Apply a natural oil finish to the coffee table, following the manufacturer's instructions.

9. Once the finish has dried, attach the hairpin legs to the bottom of the coffee table using screws.

Your coffee table is now complete and ready for use!

Desks

Designing and producing a desk is an excellent woodworking project for anyone interested in creating functional furniture pieces. In this section, we will discuss the steps involved in designing and producing desks, as well as provide a practical plan for producing them.

1. Determine the Purpose of the Desk:

The first step in designing a desk is to determine its intended purpose. Will it be used as a work desk or a writing desk? Will it be a standing desk or a sitting desk? Once you have identified the desk's intended purpose, you can begin to consider the design elements that will best suit its function.

2. Sketch Your Design:

The next step is to sketch your desk design on paper or using digital tools like SketchUp or Fusion 360. It's important to consider the dimensions of the desk, including the height, width, and depth. Sketching the design will also allow you to experiment with different shapes and configurations, ensuring that the final product is both functional and aesthetically pleasing.

3. Select Your Materials:

Once you have finalized your design, you can begin to select the materials for the desk. Common materials for desks include hardwoods like oak and maple, plywood, MDF, and particleboard. The choice of materials will depend on your budget, the desk's intended use, and your personal preferences.

4. Prepare Your Materials:

Before you begin assembling the desk, you will need to prepare the materials. This may involve cutting the wood to the correct dimensions, sanding the surfaces, and applying a finish like varnish or paint.

5. Assemble Your Desk:

The final step is to assemble the desk. This may involve using traditional joinery techniques like dovetails or mortise and tenon joints, or modern techniques like pocket hole joinery or biscuits. It's important to follow the design plan carefully to ensure that the desk is structurally sound and will last for years to come.

Practical Plan for Producing a Desk

Here is a practical plan for producing a simple but functional desk using plywood:

Materials Needed:

- 3/4" plywood sheets

- 1x3" pine boards

- Screws

- Wood glue

- Sandpaper

- Paint or varnish

Tools Needed:

- Circular saw or table saw

- Drill

- Jigsaw

- Clamps

- Tape measure

- Pencil

Steps:

1. Cut the plywood sheets to the following dimensions:

- Desktop: 30"x60"

- Side panels: 30"x28"

- Back panel: 60"x28"

- Front panel: 58.5"x6"

2. Cut the pine boards to the following dimensions:

- Legs: 28" (x4)

- Apron: 53"x3" (x2)

- Crossbar: 25"x3" (x1)

3. Sand all the surfaces of the plywood and pine boards until smooth.

4. Glue and screw the apron boards to the underside of the desktop, flush with the edges.

5. Glue and screw the legs to the apron boards, using clamps to hold them in place while the glue dries.

6. Glue and screw the crossbar to the legs, approximately 3" from the bottom.

7. Attach the side panels to the legs using glue and screws, ensuring that they are flush with the top of the crossbar.

8. Attach the back panel to the legs and side panels, using glue and screws.

9. Attach the front panel to the legs and side panels, using glue and screws.

10. Sand all the surfaces of the desk until smooth, then apply a finish of your choice (paint or varnish).

11. Let the finish dry completely, then add any additional features or accessories as desired, such as a keyboard tray or cable management system.

12. Your desk is now complete and ready to use!

Designing and producing a desk requires careful consideration of its intended purpose, materials selection, and assembly techniques. With the right tools and techniques, anyone can create a functional and beautiful desks.

Chairs

A well-designed and well-crafted chair not only serves its intended purpose but can also be an artistic piece that enhances the aesthetic of a space. Here, we will explore the steps involved in designing and producing chairs, as well as a practical plan for producing them.

Step 1: Define the Purpose of the Chair

The first step in designing a chair is to define its intended purpose. Is it going to be a dining chair, a lounge chair, or an accent chair? The intended use of the chair will dictate its design and construction. For example, a dining chair will require a different seat height and backrest angle than a lounge chair.

Step 2: Determine the Style of the Chair

The style of the chair should be in line with its intended use and the overall aesthetic of the space where it will be used. There are many styles to choose from, including modern, traditional, and rustic. The style will dictate the type of wood, joinery, and finishing techniques used.

Step 3: Sketch the Design

Once the purpose and style of the chair have been determined, it's time to sketch the design. A rough sketch can be drawn by hand, or a computer-aided design (CAD) software can be used. The design should include dimensions, joinery details, and any other pertinent information.

Step 4: Choose the Wood

The type of wood used will depend on the style of the chair and the intended use. Common woods used in chair-making include oak, cherry, walnut, and maple. Hardwoods are preferred because of their durability and strength.

Step 5: Cut the Wood

Once the design and wood have been chosen, it's time to start cutting the wood. The wood should be cut according to the dimensions specified in the design. It's important to use precise cuts to ensure that the chair fits together properly.

Step 6: Join the Pieces

The pieces of wood can be joined using a variety of techniques, including mortise and tenon, dowels, and biscuits. The joinery should be strong enough to support the weight of a person sitting on the chair. It's important to use clamps to hold the pieces in place while the glue dries.

Step 7: Sand and Finish the Chair

Once the chair is fully assembled, it's time to sand and finish it. Sanding should be done with progressively finer grits of sandpaper to ensure a smooth surface. The chair can be finished with a variety of techniques, including staining, oiling, and lacquering.

Practical Plan for Producing Chairs

Materials Needed:

- Wood

- Woodworking tools (saw, drill, chisels, clamps)

- Sandpaper

- Finishing materials (stain, oil, lacquer)

Steps:

1. Define the purpose and style of the chair.

2. Sketch the design and determine the dimensions.

3. Choose the wood and purchase the necessary materials.

4. Cut the wood according to the dimensions specified in the design.

5. Join the pieces using the chosen joinery technique.

6. Sand the chair with progressively finer grits of sandpaper.

7. Finish the chair using the chosen finishing technique.

It's important to take your time and ensure that each step is done correctly to produce a high-quality chair. With practice and patience, you can create beautiful and functional chairs that will last for generations.

Beds

Designing and producing a bed can be a great project for you as a woodworking enthusiast or professional. Beds are an essential piece of furniture that can be found in every home. They provide a comfortable and secure place for us to rest and rejuvenate. A well-crafted bed can not only serve its purpose but also enhance the beauty of your bedroom.

Here are the steps to design and produce a bed:

Step 1: Decide on the bed size and style

Before starting the project, you need to decide on the size and style of the bed. The size of the bed should depend on the space available in your bedroom and your height. You can choose from various bed sizes, such as twin, full, queen, and king.

The style of the bed should match your personal preference and the decor of your room. There are different bed styles such as platform beds, sleigh beds, four-poster beds, and panel beds.

Step 2: Choose the wood for the bed

The next step is to choose the type of wood you want to use for the bed. You can use hardwoods like oak, cherry, maple, or mahogany, or softwoods like pine or spruce. Hardwoods are more durable and attractive but are also more expensive. Softwoods are cheaper but can be prone to scratches and dents.

Step 3: Sketch a plan for the bed

Once you have decided on the size, style, and wood, it's time to sketch a plan for the bed. You can use pencil and paper or any woodworking software to draw a plan. The plan should include the dimensions, the design, and the materials needed.

Step 4: Gather the materials and tools

Based on the plan, you can now gather the necessary materials and tools. The materials will include the wood, screws, bolts, and any other hardware needed. The tools will include a saw, drill, sandpaper, measuring tape, and a level.

Step 5: Cut and shape the wood

Using the saw, you can cut the wood according to the plan. Make sure to measure accurately and cut precisely.

You can use sandpaper to smoothen the edges and shape the wood to the desired form.

Step 6: Assemble the bed frame

Now it's time to assemble the bed frame. Follow the plan and connect the pieces using screws, bolts, and other hardware. Make sure to check the level and adjust accordingly.

Step 7: Finish the bed

The final step is to finish the bed. You can use a stain, paint, or varnish to protect and enhance the wood's beauty. Allow the finish to dry completely before using the bed.

Practical Plan for Producing a Twin-Sized Platform Bed

Materials needed:

- Four pieces of 1x10x96 inch hardwood

- Two pieces of 2x4x96 inch hardwood

- 2-inch wood screws

- Sandpaper

- Wood stain

- Wood sealer

Tools needed:

- Saw

- Drill

- Measuring tape

- Level

Steps:

1. Cut the four pieces of 1x10x96 inch hardwood into two pieces of 1x10x80 inch and four pieces of 1x10x15 inch.

2. Cut the two pieces of 2x4x96 inch hardwood into four pieces of 2x4x18 inch.

3. Sand all the pieces to smoothen the edges and remove any rough spots.

4. Using the four pieces of 1x10x80 inch hardwood, assemble the frame of the bed by attaching them with 2-inch wood screws. Make sure the corners are square and the frame is level.

5. Attach the four pieces of 2x4x18 inch hardwood to the inside of the frame, making sure they are flush with the top of the frame. These will serve as support for the slats.

6. Lay the four pieces of 1x10x15 inch hardwood slats evenly across the frame, leaving about a 2-inch gap between each slat. Secure them in place with 2-inch wood screws.

7. Sand the entire bed frame and slats to remove any rough spots and to prepare for finishing.

8. Apply a coat of wood stain to the bed frame and slats, following the manufacturer's instructions. Allow the stain to dry completely.

9. Apply a coat of wood sealer to protect the wood and enhance its beauty. Allow the sealer to dry completely.

10. Your platform bed is now ready to use!

Note: This is just one example of a practical plan for a twin-sized platform bed. You can customize the design and dimensions based on your preference and needs. Make sure to follow safety guidelines and wear protective gear when working with tools and materials. With patience and careful attention to detail, you can create a beautiful and functional bed that will impress people who see it.

Cabinets

Cabinets come in various styles and sizes, ranging from small wall-mounted medicine cabinets to large free-standing kitchen cabinets. Regardless of the size or style, there are several steps involved in designing and producing cabinets.

Step 1: Design the Cabinet

The first step is to determine the design of the cabinet. This includes deciding on the size, style, and type of wood to use. It is essential to have accurate measurements of the space where the cabinet will be placed to ensure it fits perfectly. There are different cabinet styles to choose from, such as Shaker-style cabinets, raised panel cabinets, and flat panel cabinets. Each style has its unique features, so it is essential to research and select the style that suits your needs.

Step 2: Create a Plan

Once you have a design in mind, the next step is to create a plan. The plan should include a detailed list of all the materials needed, including the type of wood, hardware, and any other components needed to complete the cabinet. The plan should also include a cutting list, which specifies the dimensions of each piece of wood needed for the cabinet. A detailed plan helps ensure that the project runs smoothly and that you have all the necessary materials on hand.

Step 3: Choose the Right Wood

The type of wood you choose for your cabinet is essential. Hardwoods such as oak, maple, and cherry are popular choices because they are durable, sturdy, and have an attractive grain pattern. Softwoods like pine, spruce, and fir are also good options for cabinets because they are more affordable and easier to work with. When selecting wood, it is essential to consider the color, grain pattern, and texture of the wood, as this will affect the overall appearance of the cabinet.

Step 4: Cut the Wood

Once you have your plan and materials, it's time to start cutting the wood. Accurate cuts are essential for ensuring that the cabinet fits together correctly. A table saw or circular saw is typically used to make straight cuts, while a jigsaw or band saw is used for curved cuts. It is essential to take your time and measure twice before making any cuts to ensure that they are accurate.

Step 5: Assemble the Cabinet

After cutting the wood, it is time to start assembling the cabinet. Begin by assembling the cabinet carcass or frame, which is the basic structure of the cabinet. Use wood glue and clamps to hold the pieces together and allow the glue to dry completely. Once the frame is complete, install the cabinet doors and drawers. Cabinet doors are typically attached using hinges, while drawers are installed using drawer slides.

Step 6: Sand and Finish the Cabinet

Once the cabinet is assembled, it's time to sand and finish it. Sand the wood surfaces using progressively finer grits of sandpaper until they are smooth. The final finish will depend on personal preference and the type of wood used. Options include painting, staining, or applying a clear coat of varnish or lacquer.

Practical Plan for Producing a Basic Wall-Mounted Medicine Cabinet

Materials:

- 1/2-inch plywood (2 feet x 4 feet)

- 1/4-inch plywood (2 feet x 4 feet)

- 1x2-inch board (8 feet long)

- Wood glue

- Finishing nails

- Hinges

- Knob or handle

- Sandpaper

- Paint or stain

Tools:

- Table saw or circular saw

- Jigsaw or band saw

- Drill

- Screwdriver

- Hammer

- Clamps

Cutting List:

- Back: 18 inches x 24 inches (1/2-inch plywood)

- Top/bottom: 18 inches x 4 1/2 inches (1/2-inch plywood)

- Sides: 24 inches x 4 1/2 inches (1/2-inch plywood)

- Shelves: 16 inches x 3 1/2 inches (1/4-inch plywood) - 2 pieces

- Face frame pieces: 1x2-inch board cut to the following lengths:

- 2 pieces 18 inches long

- 2 pieces 22 1/2 inches long

Assembly Steps:

1. Begin by cutting all the wood pieces according to the cutting list using a table saw or circular saw and a jigsaw or band saw for the curved pieces.

2. Next, assemble the cabinet carcass or frame by attaching the sides to the back using wood glue and finishing nails. Use clamps to hold the pieces in place while the glue dries.

3. Once the frame is complete, attach the top and bottom pieces using wood glue and finishing nails.

4. Install the shelves inside the cabinet using wood glue and finishing nails.

5. Install the face frame pieces onto the front of the cabinet using wood glue and finishing nails. Use clamps to hold the pieces in place while the glue dries.

6. Sand the cabinet surfaces using progressively finer grits of sandpaper until they are smooth.

7. Apply the finish of your choice, such as paint or stain, following the manufacturer's instructions.

8. Attach the hinges to the cabinet and door, then attach the door to the cabinet. Install the knob or handle onto the door.

In sum, designing and producing cabinets requires careful planning, accurate measurements, and precise cuts. With the right tools and materials, you can create beautiful sets of cabinets. Whether you are making a small medicine cabinet or a large kitchen cabinet, the key is to take your time and pay attention to detail throughout the entire process.

A cabinet in a home

CHAPTER 5

OUTDOOR PROJECTS

Outdoor projects are a popular category in woodworking, offering a wide range of opportunities to create functional and beautiful structures that enhance the beauty and functionality of outdoor spaces. These projects are typically designed to withstand the elements, making them ideal for use in gardens, patios, and other outdoor areas.

Some of the most common outdoor projects include garden benches, tables, chairs, and other outdoor furniture. These pieces are often made of durable materials such as hardwoods, cedar, and teak, which can withstand exposure to moisture, UV radiation, and other environmental factors. Outdoor furniture is typically designed to be both aesthetically pleasing and comfortable, providing a comfortable place to sit and enjoy the scenery.

Another popular category of outdoor projects is outdoor structures such as pergolas, arbors, and trellises. These structures are often used to provide shade or support for climbing plants, and they can add a distinctive architectural element to a garden or patio. Pergolas and arbors can be constructed from a variety of materials, including wood, metal, and vinyl, and can be designed in a range of styles to suit any aesthetic preference.

Decking and fencing are also popular outdoor woodworking projects. Decks provide a versatile outdoor living space that can be used for entertaining, dining, and relaxation. Fencing is often used to provide privacy, security, or to enclose a garden or outdoor area. Both decking and fencing can be constructed from a variety of materials, including wood, composite materials, and metal.

Other outdoor woodworking projects include birdhouses, planters, and garden sheds. These projects can add a decorative element to a garden or patio, as well as providing functional benefits such as storage or shelter for plants and animals.

Overall, outdoor woodworking projects offer a wide range of opportunities to create beautiful and functional structures that enhance the beauty and functionality of outdoor spaces. With a little bit of creativity and skill, woodworking enthusiasts can design and build a wide variety of outdoor projects that will provide enjoyment and utility for years to come.

Decks

Designing and producing decks can be a rewarding woodworking project that requires careful planning and attention to detail. A deck is essentially a flat platform constructed outdoors, typically attached to the house and designed for outdoor living, entertaining, and relaxation. Decks can vary in size and shape depending on the space available, and can be made from a variety of materials, including wood, composite decking, and PVC.

Here are some steps to consider when designing and producing a deck:

1. Determine the size and shape of your deck

Before starting the project, it is important to decide on the size and shape of your deck. Consider the available space, the intended use, and any existing structures or obstacles. Sketch out a rough plan to visualize the final product.

2. Choose the type of material:

Select the type of material that will be used to build the deck. Wood is the most common option, and it comes in a variety of types such as cedar, redwood, and pressure-treated pine. Composite decking is also an option, which is made from a combination of plastic and wood fibers. PVC decking is another option, which is made entirely of plastic.

3. Prepare the site:

Clear the site where the deck will be built. Remove any existing structures, trees, or plants that are in the way. Level the ground if necessary and mark the boundaries of the deck with stakes and string.

4. Build the foundation:

A deck foundation is typically made up of posts and beams that will support the weight of the deck. Dig holes for the posts, and pour concrete footings into the holes. Then, install the posts and beams to create a sturdy framework for the deck.

5. Install the decking:

After the foundation is complete, install the decking boards on top of the framework. Use screws or nails to attach the boards to the beams, making sure they are spaced evenly and securely fastened.

6. Add railing and stairs:

Railing is necessary to ensure safety, and stairs are needed if the deck is raised off the ground. Install railings around the perimeter of the deck and stairs to provide access to the deck.

7. Finish the deck:

Finally, finish the deck with a protective coating or stain. This will help to protect the wood from the elements and keep it looking new for longer.

In terms of a practical plan, here is an example of a deck plan:

- Size: 16 feet by 20 feet

- Material: Pressure-treated pine

- Foundation: Four posts, each 4 feet deep with concrete footings

- Beams: Two beams, each 16 feet long

- Joists: 16 joists, each 20 feet long

- Decking: 2x6 decking boards, spaced 1/8 inch apart

- Railing: Two 4-foot sections of railing

- Stairs: One 4-step staircase

To produce this deck, follow these steps:

1. Clear the site of any obstacles, and mark the boundaries of the deck with stakes and string.

2. Dig four holes for the posts, each 4 feet deep. Pour concrete footings into the holes and allow them to dry.

3. Install the four posts into the concrete footings, making sure they are level.

4. Install two beams across the top of the posts, attaching them with metal brackets.

5. Attach 16 joists across the beams, spaced evenly.

6. Install the 2x6 decking boards perpendicular to the joists, leaving a 1/8 inch gap between each board.

7. Install the railing along the perimeter of the deck, attaching it to the posts with metal brackets.

8. Install the stairs at one end of the deck, attaching them to the beams and the joists.

9. Finish the deck with a protective coating or stain to prevent water damage and to give it a finished look.

Please note that the design and production of decks require proper safety precautions. Always wear appropriate protective gear such as gloves, safety glasses, and a dust mask when handling wood and power tools. Also, make sure to follow the manufacturer's instructions for all tools and materials used in the project.

Gazebos

A gazebo is a beautiful outdoor structure that provides a comfortable and inviting space for relaxation and entertainment. Gazebos are typically built in parks, gardens, and outdoor spaces where people gather for events such as weddings, picnics, and outdoor parties. Gazebos can be designed and produced in a variety of styles, shapes, and sizes to suit different preferences and functional needs. Shortly, we will look at how to design and produce gazebos, and also provide a practical plan for producing them.

A Gazebo

Designing Gazebos

1. Purpose: The first step in designing a gazebo is to determine its purpose. Will it be used for outdoor dining, relaxation, or entertaining guests? The purpose of the gazebo will determine the size, shape, and features that it should have.

2. Location: The location of the gazebo is also important. It should be placed in a spot that is easily accessible and provides a good view of the surrounding landscape. The gazebo should also be situated in a place that gets plenty of natural light and ventilation.

3. Style: Gazebos can be designed in a variety of styles, from traditional to modern. Some popular styles include Victorian, Colonial, and Asian-inspired designs. The style of the gazebo should complement the architecture and landscaping of the surrounding area.

4. Size: The size of the gazebo will depend on its purpose and the number of people it will accommodate. A small gazebo may be sufficient for intimate gatherings, while a larger gazebo may be needed for larger events.

5. Materials: Gazebos can be made from a variety of materials, including wood, metal, and vinyl. Wood is a

popular choice because it is durable, attractive, and can be stained or painted to match the surrounding area.

6. Features: Gazebos can be designed with a variety of features, such as benches, tables, and lighting. The features that are included will depend on the purpose of the gazebo and the budget.

Producing Gazebos

a. Planning: The first step in producing gazebos is to create a plan. The plan should include a detailed list of materials, tools, and supplies that will be needed, as well as a timeline for completing the project.

b. Cutting the wood: Once the plan is in place, the wood can be cut to the desired size and shape. Careful attention should be paid to the accuracy of the cuts, as any mistakes can affect the stability of the structure.

c. Assembly: The pieces of wood can be assembled using nails or screws. It is important to use the right type of fastener for the job, as using the wrong type can cause the wood to split or crack.

d. Finishing: Once the gazebo is assembled, it can be finished with paint or stain. This will help to protect the wood from the elements and give it an attractive appearance.

e. Adding Features: After the gazebo is finished, any additional features such as benches, tables, and lighting can be added. These features should be carefully chosen to complement the design and purpose of the gazebo.

Practical Plan for Producing Gazebos

Materials:

- 4x4x8 pressure-treated lumber

- 2x4x8 pressure-treated lumber

- 1x6x8 pressure-treated lumber

- Roofing material (shingles or metal)

- Nails and screws

- Concrete mix

Tools:

- Circular saw

- Drill

- Hammer

- Shovel

- Level

Steps:

1. Determine the size and style of the gazebo.

2. Mark out the location of the gazebo and prepare the ground by digging a hole and filling it with concrete.

3. Cut the 4x4x8 lumber into pieces of equal length, based on the size of the gazebo. These will be used as the posts.

4. Cut the 2x4x8 lumber into pieces that will be used to create the roof structure and the bracing for the posts.

5.

6. Assemble the posts by attaching the 2x4s to each side of the post, forming an "L" shape.

7. Dig holes for the posts and set them in place with concrete.

8. Attach the crossbeams to the top of the posts, creating a square or rectangular frame.

9. Cut the 1x6x8 lumber into pieces and attach them to the roof structure to form the roof decking.

10. Install the roofing material over the decking, using shingles or metal roofing.

11. Add any additional features such as benches or tables, and finish the gazebo with paint or stain.

Designing and producing gazebos requires careful planning, attention to detail, and skilled woodworking. By following the steps outlined in this chapter, you can create a beautiful and functional outdoor structure that will provide years of enjoyment for you and your guests. Remember to choose the right materials, tools, and features that will meet your needs and complement the surrounding landscape. With a little patience and hard work, you can create a stunning gazebo that will be the envy of your neighborhood.

Fences

Designing and producing fences can be a great woodworking project for those who are looking to develop their skills in carpentry. Fences are useful structures that provide privacy, security, and decoration to any property. Whether you want to build a simple picket fence for your garden or a sturdy fence to keep your livestock safe, the process involves careful planning, attention to detail, and the use of proper tools and materials.

Here are the steps to follow to design and produce a fence:

Step 1: Determine the purpose and style of your fence

The first step in designing your fence is to determine its purpose and style. Do you want a fence to provide privacy, security, or decoration? Would you like a fence that complements the architecture of your home or landscape? Once you have identified the purpose and style of your fence, you can start sketching some ideas.

Step 2: Measure the area

Measure the area where you plan to build your fence. This will help you determine the amount of materials you will need to purchase. Measure the length and width of the fence, and consider the height you want your fence to be.

Step 3: Choose your materials

The next step is to choose your materials. Depending on the purpose and style of your fence, you can choose from a variety of materials such as wood, metal, vinyl, or composite. Wood is a popular choice for fencing because it is versatile, durable, and aesthetically pleasing. Cedar, redwood, and pine are common types of wood used for fencing.

Step 4: Plan your design

Once you have chosen your materials, it's time to plan your design. Sketch out your fence design on paper, including the dimensions and materials you plan to use. Take into account any obstacles, such as trees or rocks, that may affect the placement and design of your fence.

Step 5: Prepare the area

Before you start building your fence, you need to prepare the area. Clear the ground of any debris or vegetation, and mark the location of any underground utilities, such as gas, water, or electric lines.

Step 6: Build the fence

Now it's time to build your fence. Start by measuring and cutting your posts to the correct height. Use a post hole digger to dig holes for your posts, and place them in the holes, making sure they are level and plumb. Next, attach your rails to the posts, and then attach your pickets to the rails. Finally, add any decorative elements, such as post caps or lattice work.

Step 7: Finish the fence

Once your fence is built, you can finish it with a protective coat of stain or paint to help protect it from the elements.

A wooden fence

Here comes a practical plan for producing a wood fence:

Materials:

- Cedar fence pickets

- Cedar 2x4s

- Cedar 4x4s

- Galvanized nails or screws

- Concrete mix

- Stain or paint

Tools:

- Circular saw

- Post hole digger

- Level

- Drill

- Hammer

- Tape measure

Design:

A 6-foot-tall picket fence with a flat top and no decorative elements.

Instructions:

1. Measure the area where you plan to build your fence.

2. Purchase your materials, including the correct number of fence pickets, 2x4s, and 4x4s.

3. Use a post hole digger to dig holes for your 4x4s. Space the holes evenly, according to the length of your fence.

4. Place a 4x4 in each hole and fill the hole with concrete mix. Use a level to make sure the posts are plumb and level. Allow the concrete to dry for at least 24 hours.

5. Once the concrete has dried, measure and cut your 2x4s to fit between the posts, leaving a gap of about 1/2 inch between each board.

6. Attach the 2x4s to the posts using galvanized nails or screws. Make sure they are level and plumb.

7. Measure and cut your fence pickets to the correct length. You can either cut them to a uniform length or create a staggered pattern for a more natural look.

8. Attach the fence pickets to the rails using galvanized nails or screws. Space them evenly, leaving a gap of about 1/2 inch between each picket.

9. Once all the pickets are attached, trim any excess length off the tops of the pickets to create a flat top.

10. Apply a protective coat of stain or paint to the fence to help protect it from the elements.

11. Optional: add decorative elements such as post caps or lattice work to the top of the fence for added visual appeal.

With these steps, you can successfully design and produce a beautiful and functional fence that will enhance the look of your property while providing privacy and security. Just remember to take your time, pay attention to detail, and use the right tools and materials for the job.

Benches

Designing and producing benches is a great woodworking project for both beginners and experienced woodworkers.

Benches come in a wide variety of styles and can serve different purposes, from garden benches to indoor seating. In this article, we will explore the steps involved in designing and producing benches and provide a practical plan for producing them.

Step 1: Determine the Purpose of the Bench

The first step in designing and producing benches is to determine the purpose of the bench. This will determine the size, style, and materials you will need for the project. For example, if you are designing an outdoor garden bench, you will need to choose materials that are weather-resistant, such as cedar or redwood. On the other hand, if you are designing an indoor bench, you may choose softer woods like pine or maple.

Step 2: Choose the Style of the Bench

Once you have determined the purpose of the bench, you can begin to choose the style of the bench. There are many different styles of benches, from traditional to modern. Some popular styles include Adirondack, Chippendale, and Mission. Consider the style of your home or garden when choosing the style of your bench.

Step 3: Create a Sketch or Plan

The next step is to create a sketch or plan for your bench. This will help you visualize the finished product and determine the materials and tools you will need. You can create a simple sketch on paper or use a woodworking software program to create a more detailed plan.

Step 4: Choose the Materials

Once you have a plan for your bench, you can begin to choose the materials you will need. The type of wood you choose will depend on the purpose and style of your bench. Other materials you may need include screws, nails, glue, and paint or stain.

Step 5: Cut the Wood

After you have chosen your materials, it's time to cut the wood. Use your plan to determine the dimensions of each piece of wood and mark them accordingly. Use a saw to cut the wood to the correct size.

Step 6: Sand the Wood

After cutting the wood, you will need to sand it to create a smooth surface. Use a sandpaper with a fine grit to sand the wood. This will prepare it for staining or painting.

Step 7: Assemble the Bench

Now it's time to assemble the bench. Use your plan to determine the order in which to assemble the pieces. Use screws or nails to secure the pieces together.

Step 8: Stain or Paint the Bench

Finally, you can stain or paint the bench to give it the desired finish. Choose a stain or paint that is appropriate for the type of wood you used. Apply the stain or paint with a brush or roller, following the manufacturer's instructions.

Practical Plan for Producing a Bench

Materials:

- 2x4 wood boards

- 1x4 wood boards

- screws

- wood glue

- wood stain or paint

Tools:

- saw

- drill

- screwdriver

- sander

- paintbrush or roller

Step 1: Cut the Wood

Cut the following pieces of wood:

- 4 legs (2x4, 16 inches long)

- 2 seat supports (2x4, 40 inches long)

- 2 armrest supports (2x4, 25 inches long)

- 4 seat slats (1x4, 40 inches long)

- 2 armrests (1x4, 25 inches long)

- 2 backrests (1x4, 30 inches long)

- 4 backrest slats (1x4, 30 inches long)

Step 2: Sand the Wood

Sand all of the wood pieces to create a smooth surface. Start with a coarse grit sandpaper and finish with a fine grit sandpaper. Sand the edges and corners to round them off.

Step 3: Assemble the Bench Frame

Attach the seat supports to the legs using screws and wood glue. Then, attach the armrest supports to the legs using screws and wood glue. Make sure the supports are level and flush with the legs.

Step 4: Install the Seat Slats

Attach the seat slats to the seat supports using screws and wood glue. Space the slats evenly and make sure they are level.

Step 5: Install the Armrests and Backrests

Attach the armrests to the armrest supports using screws and wood glue. Attach the backrests to the back of the armrests using screws and wood glue. Then, attach the backrest slats to the backrest using screws and wood glue. Space the slats evenly and make sure they are level.

Step 6: Sand and Finish the Bench

Sand the entire bench to create a smooth surface. Then, apply wood stain or paint to the bench using a paintbrush or roller. Allow the finish to dry completely.

Step 7: Enjoy Your New Bench!

Your bench is now complete and ready to be used! Place it in your garden or on your patio, and enjoy the beauty and functionality of your new piece of furniture.

Remember to take your time, follow the steps carefully, and enjoy the process!

CHAPTER 6

SMALL WOODWORKING PROJECTS

Small woodworking projects are a great way to practice and develop woodworking skills while creating useful and beautiful objects. These projects typically require less time, materials, and tools than larger projects, making them ideal for beginners or those with limited space or resources.

Small woodworking projects can include anything from simple boxes and picture frames to decorative shelves, kitchen utensils, and even furniture. They can be made from a variety of materials, including wood, metal, and plastic, but wood is the most popular choice due to its natural beauty and versatility.

One of the advantages of this type of projects is that they can be completed relatively quickly, often in just a few hours or days, which can provide a sense of accomplishment and satisfaction. Additionally, these projects allow woodworkers to experiment with different techniques, tools, and finishes without committing to a larger, more complex project.

Small woodworking projects can also be a great way to use up scraps of wood that might otherwise go to waste. Many woodworkers keep a collection of small pieces of wood on hand specifically for these types of projects, and some even specialize in creating small items using only scrap wood.

Overall, small woodworking projects offer a fun and rewarding way to hone woodworking skills and create beautiful and functional objects. They are accessible to woodworkers of all skill levels and can be a great way to explore new techniques and materials.

Birdhouses

A creative and rewarding woodworking activity is designing and building birdhouses. Building birdhouses enables you to refine your abilities and produce something that is both practical and visually beautiful, regardless of whether you are an expert carpenter or a beginner. This manual will lead you through the procedures involved in designing and building birdhouses, including the choice of materials, the equipment required, and safety precautions. I'll also provide a practical plan for producing a simple, yet elegant birdhouse.

A birdhouse

Materials Selection:

The first step in designing and producing a birdhouse is selecting the right materials. When it comes to birdhouses, you'll want to choose wood that's both durable and safe for birds. Cedar and redwood are popular choices due to their durability and natural resistance to decay and insect damage. Pine and fir are also options, but they may require additional treatments to protect them from the elements.

When selecting wood for your birdhouse, make sure to choose pieces that are free of knots, cracks, and other defects that could weaken the structure. You'll also want to select wood that's at least ¾-inch thick to provide sufficient insulation for the birds.

Tools Needed:

Once you've selected your wood, you'll need a variety of tools to build your birdhouse. Here's a list of the most essential tools:

- Table saw or circular saw

- Miter saw or hand saw

- Drill

- Jigsaw or coping saw

- Screwdriver

- Clamps

- Sandpaper

Safety Considerations:

Working with wood can be dangerous, so it's important to take the necessary safety precautions. Make sure to wear eye protection, ear protection, and a dust mask when cutting, sanding, or drilling wood. Also, make sure to use sharp blades and bits to reduce the risk of kickback or other accidents.

Design Plan

Here's a simple plan for a birdhouse that's both easy to build and functional:

Materials Needed:

- 1 piece of cedar, redwood, or pine, 8 inches wide by 5 feet long and ¾-inch thick

- 1 ½-inch wood screws

- 1 1/8-inch drill bit

- Sandpaper

Instructions:

1. Cut the wood into the following pieces:

2. One 8-inch by 8-inch square for the floor

3. Two 6-inch by 8-inch rectangles for the sides

4. One 6-inch by 6-inch square for the back

5. One 8-inch by 6-inch rectangle for the roof

6. Two 2-inch by 6-inch rectangles for the front and back of the roof

7. Two 1 ½-inch by 1 ½-inch squares for the perch

8. Use the 1 1/8-inch drill bit to drill a 1 ½-inch entrance hole in the center of the front piece, about 1 inch from the top.

9. Sand all the pieces to remove any rough edges or splinters.

10. Assemble the birdhouse by attaching the sides to the floor using wood screws. Then attach the back to the sides using wood screws.

11. Attach the front of the roof to the sides and back using wood screws. Then attach the back of the roof to the sides and back using wood screws.

12. Attach the perch to the front of the birdhouse, just below the entrance hole, using wood screws.

13. Finally, attach a hanger to the top of the roof to hang the birdhouse from a tree or other structure.

Building birdhouses is a great way to practice your woodworking skills while providing a safe and comfortable home for our feathered friends. By following the tips and plan provided above, you'll be able to design and produce a beautiful and functional birdhouse that will provide years of enjoyment for both you and the birds. Remember to always prioritize safety when working with wood, and choose high-quality materials that are safe for birds. With a little creativity and effort, you can create a unique birdhouse that not only looks great but also provides a safe and cozy home for birds to raise their young. So grab your tools, get to work, and let your love for woodworking and birds soar!

Clocks

Designing and producing clocks can be a rewarding woodworking project that requires precision, attention to detail, and patience. In this guide, we will cover the steps you need to follow to design and produce a clock, including selecting materials, choosing a design, cutting and shaping the pieces, and assembling and finishing the clock.

Selecting Materials

The first step in designing a clock is to select the appropriate materials. You will need to decide on the type of wood you will use, the type of clock mechanism you will use, and any additional materials such as glass or metal accents. The type of wood you choose will depend on your budget, the final appearance you want to achieve, and the durability you need. Common woods used in clock making include oak, maple, cherry, and walnut.

Choosing a Design

Once you have selected your materials, you will need to choose a clock design. This can range from a simple round wall clock to a more complex grandfather clock. There are many resources available online for clock designs, and you can also consider designing your own. Consider factors such as the size of the clock, the placement of the clock face and hands, and any additional features such as pendulums or chimes.

Cutting and Shaping the Pieces

Once you have selected your materials and design, it's time to start cutting and shaping the pieces. This will involve using a combination of hand tools and power tools such as a saw, drill, and router. It's important to take your time and measure twice before making any cuts to avoid mistakes. Consider using a template or pattern to help guide your cuts and ensure consistency in the size and shape of each piece.

Assembling the Clock

Once you have cut and shaped all of the pieces, it's time to assemble the clock. This will involve attaching the clock mechanism to the clock face, attaching any additional features such as a pendulum or chimes, and securing the glass or metal accents. Follow the instructions provided with the clock mechanism to ensure proper assembly.

Finishing the Clock

The final step in producing a clock is to finish it. This will involve sanding the wood to a smooth finish, staining or painting the wood to achieve the desired color, and applying a protective coat of varnish or polyurethane. Take your time and apply multiple coats of varnish or polyurethane to ensure a durable and long-lasting finish.

Here is a practical plan for producing a simple round wall clock:

Materials:

- 1 12-inch round piece of wood

- 1 clock mechanism kit

- Sandpaper (120-grit and 220-grit)

- Stain or paint

- Varnish or polyurethane

- Paintbrushes

- Drill with a 3/8-inch bit

- Saw

Instructions:

1. Cut a 12-inch round piece of wood using a saw.

2. Sand the wood using 120-grit sandpaper, then repeat with 220-grit sandpaper.

3. Apply a coat of stain or paint to the wood using a paintbrush, then allow it to dry completely.

4. Apply a coat of varnish or polyurethane to the wood using a paintbrush, then allow it to dry completely.

5. Mark the center of the wood with a pencil.

6. Use a drill with a 3/8-inch bit to drill a hole in the center of the wood.

7. Insert the clock mechanism kit into the hole, following the instructions provided with the kit.

8. Attach the clock hands to the mechanism, following the instructions provided with the kit.

9. Hang the clock on the wall using a picture hanger or wall hook.

Designing and producing clocks requires careful consideration of materials, design, and assembly. With patience and attention to detail, a clock can become a functional and decorative piece that will be cherished for years to come. Remember to take your time during each step of the process, measure twice before making any cuts, and follow instructions carefully to ensure proper assembly. Irrespective of whether you choose to create a simple round wall clock or a more complex grandfather clock, the satisfaction of creating a handmade timepiece will make it all worthwhile. Happy woodworking!

Toys

Designing and producing toys can be a fun and rewarding project for those interested in woodworking. Whether you are making toys for your own children or for commercial purposes, there are a few important considerations to keep in mind to ensure your toys are safe, durable, and enjoyable for children to play with.

1. Choose a Safe and Appropriate Design:

When designing your toys, safety should be your top priority. Make sure that any toys you create are age-appropriate and do not pose a choking hazard. If you are unsure about the safety of a design, it is always best to err on the side of caution and choose a different design.

2. Select the Right Materials:

The type of wood you choose will have a big impact on the durability and safety of your toys. You should select a hardwood that is free of knots, cracks, and other defects that could weaken the structure of the toy. You should also avoid using softwoods, as they are more prone to splintering and breaking.

3. Use Child-Safe Finishes:

When finishing your toys, it is important to use a child-safe finish that will not leach harmful chemicals or create a choking hazard. Look for finishes that are non-toxic and can withstand the wear and tear of regular use.

4. Pay Attention to Details:

When creating your toys, pay close attention to the details. Make sure that all joints are secure and that there are no sharp edges or corners that could cause injury. Sand all surfaces smooth to avoid splinters, and use non-toxic paints and finishes to add color and personality to your toys.

Now that we've covered some of the important considerations for designing and producing toys, let's take a look at a practical plan for producing them.

Toy Production Plan

1. Choose your toy design and gather materials:

Choose a toy design that is safe, fun, and appropriate for the age group you are targeting. Once you have your design, gather all the necessary materials, including hardwood, sandpaper, saws, and child-safe finishes.

2. Cut and shape the wood:

Using a saw, cut the wood into the desired shapes and sizes for your toy. Use sandpaper to smooth out any rough edges or surfaces.

3. Assemble the toy:

Use glue or other joinery techniques to assemble the pieces of your toy. Make sure all joints are secure and that there are no sharp edges or corners that could cause injury.

4. Finish the toy:

Apply a child-safe finish to your toy to add color and protect the wood from wear and tear. Allow the finish to dry completely before allowing children to play with the toy.

5. Test the toy:

Before releasing your toy to the public, test it to make sure it is safe and durable. Make sure it can withstand the wear and tear of regular use and does not pose any choking hazards.

By following these steps and paying close attention to the details, you can create safe, fun, and durable toys that will be enjoyed by children within and outside your locality.

Bookcases

Bookcases are versatile and functional pieces of furniture that can be customized to fit any space or style. There are a few key steps to keep in mind when designing and producing bookcases.

Step 1: Determine the size and style of your bookcase

Before you begin your project, it's important to determine the size and style of your bookcase. Consider the space where the bookcase will be placed and the types of items that will be stored on it. For example, if you're planning to store large books or decorative items, you'll need a bookcase with deeper shelves.

There are many different styles of bookcases to choose from, including open shelving, closed shelving, ladder-style, and built-in bookcases. You'll want to choose a style that fits your space and your personal style.

Step 2: Choose your wood and finish

Once you've determined the size and style of your bookcase, it's time to choose the wood and finish. There are many different types of wood to choose from, including oak, pine, cherry, and walnut. Each type of wood has its own unique characteristics, so you'll want to choose a wood that fits your personal style and the style of your home.

In addition to choosing your wood, you'll also need to choose a finish. The finish will protect your bookcase from scratches and other damage, and can also enhance the natural beauty of the wood. Some popular finishes include stain, paint, and varnish.

Step 3: Create a plan and gather materials

Before you begin building your bookcase, it's important to create a detailed plan. This plan should include the size and style of your bookcase, as well as a list of materials and tools that you'll need.

Some common materials and tools for building a bookcase include:

- Wood (cut to size)
- Screws or nails
- Wood glue
- Sandpaper
- Saw
- Drill
- Measuring tape
- Level

Step 4: Cut and assemble your bookcase

Once you have your materials and tools, it's time to begin building your bookcase. Start by cutting the wood to the correct size and shape, and then assemble the shelves and sides of the bookcase using screws or nails and wood glue.

Be sure to sand the bookcase thoroughly before applying any finish. This will help to ensure a smooth and even finish.

Step 5: Apply your finish

Finally, it's time to apply your finish. This can be done using a brush, roller, or spray gun, depending on the type of finish you've chosen. Be sure to follow the manufacturer's instructions for applying the finish, and allow ample time for the finish to dry before using your bookcase.

By following these key steps and taking the time to plan and prepare, you can create a beautiful and functional piece of furniture that you'll be proud to display in your home or sell for profit.

To buttress the above points, here is a practical plan for a simple design bookcase:

Materials:

- 2x12x8 pine boards (for shelves)

- 1x6x8 pine boards (for sides and trim)

- 1x4x8 pine boards (for back)

- 2" screws

- Wood glue

- Sandpaper

- Stain or paint

Tools:

- Saw

- Drill

- Measuring tape

- Level

Instructions:

1. Cut two 1x6x8 boards to the desired height of your bookcase (usually around 6 feet).

2. Cut four 1x6x8 boards to the desired width of your bookcase (usually around 3 feet).

3. Cut two 1x4x8 boards to the same height as your side pieces.

4. Use wood glue and screws to attach the two side pieces to the top and bottom pieces.

5. Cut the 2x12x8 boards to the desired length for your shelves.

6. Attach the shelves to the sides using wood glue and screws.

7. Cut the remaining 1x4x8 boards to fit as a back panel and attach them to the back of the bookcase using wood glue and screws.

8. Sand the entire bookcase until it is smooth.

9. Apply stain or paint to the bookcase and allow it to dry completely before use.

This design is a simple and classic style that can be easily customized to fit any space or personal style. By following these steps and using high-quality materials and tools, you can create a elegant and functional bookcase that will last for years to come.

A bookcase

Shelves

Shelves are a functional and decorative woodworking project that can be customized to fit any space and style. Whether you are a beginner or an experienced woodworker, designing and producing shelves can be a rewarding and satisfying project. I will show you the steps involved in designing and producing shelves, and provide a practical plan for producing them.

Step 1: Determine the Purpose of the Shelves

The first step in designing shelves is to determine their purpose. Are you making them for storage, display, or both? Will they be used in a bedroom, living room, or kitchen? The answers to these questions will help you determine the size, shape, and style of the shelves.

Step 2: Choose the Wood

The second step is to choose the wood for your shelves. The type of wood you choose will depend on your budget, the look you want to achieve, and the durability you need. Common types of wood for shelves include oak, maple, cherry, and pine.

Step 3: Measure and Cut the Wood

The third step is to measure and cut the wood for your shelves. Use a measuring tape and a saw to cut the wood to the desired length and width. Be sure to use safety precautions when using a saw, such as wearing safety glasses and keeping your hands away from the blade.

Step 4: Sand and Finish the Wood

The fourth step is to sand and finish the wood for your shelves. Use sandpaper to smooth out any rough edges or surfaces. Then, apply a stain or finish to the wood to protect it from moisture and wear and tear.

Step 5: Assemble the Shelves

The fifth step is to assemble the shelves. This will involve attaching the shelves to brackets or supports. There are several different ways to attach shelves to supports, such as using screws or dowels.

Step 6: Install the Shelves

The final step is to install the shelves in their intended location. Use a level to ensure that the shelves are even and straight. Then, attach the shelves to the wall using screws or other hardware.

Practical Plan for Producing Shelves

Here is a practical plan for producing shelves:

Materials:

- Wood (oak, maple, cherry, or pine)

- Sandpaper

- Stain or finish

- Brackets or supports

- Screws or dowels

- Hardware for attaching shelves to the wall

Tools:

- Measuring tape

- Saw

- Drill

- Screwdriver

Instructions:

1. Determine the purpose of the shelves and choose the wood.

2. Measure and cut the wood for the shelves.

3. Sand and finish the wood.

4. Attach the shelves to brackets or supports using screws or dowels.

5. Install the shelves on the wall using hardware.

The dimensions of the shelves will depend on the size of the space and the intended use. For example, if the shelves are for storing books, you may want to make them deeper than if they are for displaying knick-knacks.

In sum, you can customize shelves to fit any space and style. By following the outlined steps and using the practical plan provided, you can create beautiful and functional shelves that will enhance your home or office.

A shelf

CHAPTER 7

WOODTURNING PROJECTS

Woodturning is the art of shaping wood using a lathe to create a wide range of decorative and functional objects. Woodturning projects offer woodworkers the opportunity to create unique pieces that can be both beautiful and useful. From small turned boxes to large bowls and furniture legs, there is no limit to the types of projects that can be created with a lathe.

One of the most popular woodturning projects is the bowl. Bowls can be made in a variety of sizes and shapes, and can be used for both decorative and practical purposes. Turning a bowl requires skill and patience, as the wood must be carefully shaped and sanded to achieve the desired form and finish. Other popular woodturning projects include pens, candlesticks, and vases.

Woodturning also offers the opportunity to create more complex pieces of furniture, such as table legs, chair spindles, and bed posts. These projects require more advanced skills and techniques, as well as a larger lathe and other specialized equipment. However, the end result can be stunning, adding a unique touch to any piece of furniture.

One of the benefits of woodturning projects is that they can be created from a wide variety of wood species, each with its own unique characteristics and beauty. Some popular woods for turning include maple, cherry, walnut, and oak. Exotic woods such as rosewood, ebony, and cocobolo can also be used for more exotic projects.

Woodturning can be a challenging and rewarding craft, requiring both technical skill and artistic creativity. However, with practice and dedication, woodworkers can create beautiful and unique pieces that will be treasured for years to come. Whether you are a seasoned woodturner or just starting out, there are endless possibilities for woodturning projects that can help you hone your skills and showcase your talent.

Bowls

Designing and producing bowls is a great woodworking project that requires a combination of creativity, skill, and attention to detail. Bowls can be made from a variety of materials, including wood, ceramic, glass, and metal, but in this guide, we will focus on designing and producing wooden bowls.

The first step in designing a wooden bowl is to choose the type of wood you want to use. Different woods have different colors, grains, and densities, which can all affect the final look and feel of your bowl. Some popular woods for bowl-making include maple, cherry, walnut, and oak.

Once you have selected your wood, you will need to decide on the shape and size of your bowl. You can either create a symmetrical bowl with a perfectly round shape or experiment with irregular shapes and asymmetrical designs. You will also need to determine the size of your bowl based on its intended use. For example, a small bowl may be ideal for serving snacks or holding jewelry, while a larger bowl could be used for serving salads or as a centerpiece on a dining table.

To create a practical plan for producing your wooden bowl, you can follow the steps below:

Step 1: Prepare the Wood

Start by selecting a piece of wood that is large enough to create your desired bowl shape. Cut the wood into a rough shape using a saw, and then use a lathe to shape the wood into a bowl shape. Use a gouge or chisel to remove any excess wood and create the bowl's desired shape.

Step 2: Hollow out the Bowl

Using a bowl gouge, begin hollowing out the center of the bowl. Start at the center and work your way outwards, carefully removing wood to create the desired depth and shape of the bowl.

Step 3: Sand the Bowl

Once the bowl is hollowed out, use sandpaper to smooth the interior and exterior surfaces of the bowl. Start with a coarse grit sandpaper and work your way up to a fine grit sandpaper to achieve a smooth finish.

Step 4: Finish the Bowl

Apply a finish to the bowl to protect the wood and enhance its natural beauty. You can choose from a variety of finishes, including oil, wax, and varnish. Apply the finish according to the manufacturer's instructions and allow the bowl to dry completely before using it.

When designing and producing your wooden bowl, keep in mind that each bowl will be unique and reflect your personal style and creativity. Experiment with different shapes, sizes, and finishes to create a bowl that is both functional and beautiful.

Pens

A well-designed wooden pen can be a beautiful and functional addition to any office or personal collection. Here, we will be looking at an overview of the design and production process for wooden pens, as well as a practical plan for producing them.

Designing the Pen

Before you begin the production process, it is important to have a clear idea of what you want your pen to look like. Consider the following design elements:

1. Pen Type: There are many types of pens to choose from, including ballpoint, fountain, and rollerball pens. Each type requires different components and assembly techniques, so it is important to decide on a pen type before proceeding.

2. Wood Type: The type of wood you choose will have a significant impact on the appearance and durability of your pen. Some common woods used for pens include maple, walnut, and rosewood.

3. Shape and Size: Pens come in a variety of shapes and sizes, so it is important to consider the overall look and feel you want your pen to have.

4. Hardware: The hardware components of a pen include the nib, ink cartridge, clip, and finial. Choose components that match the style and color scheme of your pen.

Producing the Pen

Once you have designed your pen, it is time to start production. Follow these steps to produce a wooden pen:

a. **Select and Prepare the Wood:** Choose a high-quality piece of wood that is free of knots and defects. Cut the wood to the appropriate length and diameter for your pen type.

b. **Drill the Blank:** Use a drill press to create a hole in the center of the wood blank. The diameter of the hole should match the diameter of the hardware components you will be using.

c. **Turn the Blank:** Use a lathe to turn the wood blank into the desired shape and size. Be sure to sand the wood carefully to achieve a smooth finish.

d. **Install the Hardware:** Follow the manufacturer's instructions to install the nib, ink cartridge, clip, and finial. Make sure all components are securely attached.

e. **Apply Finish:** Apply a coat of finish to the pen to protect the wood and enhance its appearance. Some common finishes include lacquer, varnish, and wax.

Practical Plan for Producing Pens

Here is a practical plan for producing a wooden pen:

Materials:

• Wood blank

• Pen kit

• Sandpaper (80-320 grit)

• Finish (lacquer, varnish, or wax)

• Lathe

• Drill press

Steps:

1. Select a high-quality piece of wood for your pen blank.

2. Cut the wood to the appropriate length and diameter for your pen type.

3. Use a drill press to create a hole in the center of the wood blank.

4. Mount the wood blank onto the lathe.

5. Turn the wood blank into the desired shape and size, using sandpaper to smooth the surface.

6. Install the hardware components according to the manufacturer's instructions.

7. Apply a coat of finish to the pen to protect the wood and enhance its appearance.

By following these steps, you can produce a beautiful and functional wooden pen that you can be proud of. With practice and experimentation, you can develop your own unique style and techniques for designing and producing wooden pens.

Spindles

Spindles are long, thin, cylindrical-shaped pieces of wood that are used in woodworking projects for a variety of purposes. They can be used as chair legs, table legs, stair balusters, and many other decorative or functional applications. Spindles can be made from a variety of wood species, and their design and production depend on the intended use and style of the final product.

Here are some steps to follow when designing and producing spindles for a woodworking project:

1. Determine the size and shape of the spindle

The first step in designing a spindle is to determine the size and shape of the finished product. Consider the intended use of the spindle and the overall design of the final product. You can use a pencil and paper or a computer-aided design (CAD) software to sketch out the shape and size of the spindle.

2. Choose the wood species

The wood species you choose for your spindle will depend on the intended use and the desired appearance of the final product. Hardwoods such as oak, maple, and cherry are popular choices for spindles, as they are strong and durable. Softwoods such as pine and cedar can also be used for spindles but may not be as durable.

3. Prepare the wood

Once you have chosen your wood species, you will need to prepare the wood for spindle production. Start by cutting the wood to the appropriate length and thickness. Use a planer or jointer to smooth and flatten the wood. You may also need to sand the wood to remove any rough spots or imperfections.

4. Mark the spindle

Mark the wood at the points where you want to create the spindle's design elements, such as beads or coves. You can use a pencil or marking gauge to make these marks.

5. Use a lathe to shape the spindle

To create the spindle's cylindrical shape and design elements, you will need to use a lathe. A lathe is a machine that rotates the wood while you use cutting tools to shape it. You can use a variety of cutting tools, including gouges, chisels, and scrapers, to create the spindle's shape and design elements.

6. Sand and finish the spindle

Once you have shaped the spindle, you will need to sand it to remove any tool marks or rough spots. Start with a coarse grit sandpaper and work your way up to a finer grit. After sanding, apply a finish to the spindle, such as stain or varnish, to protect the wood and enhance its appearance.

Here is a practical plan for producing spindles:

Materials:

• Wood of your choice

• Lathe

• Cutting tools (gouges, chisels, scrapers)

• Sandpaper (coarse and fine grits)

• Finish (stain, varnish, etc.)

Steps:

1. Cut the wood to the appropriate length and thickness.

2. Use a planer or jointer to smooth and flatten the wood.

3. Mark the wood at the points where you want to create the spindle's design elements.

4. Set up the lathe and attach the wood to the spindle.

5. Turn on the lathe and use cutting tools to shape the wood into a cylinder with the desired design elements.

6. Sand the spindle with coarse grit sandpaper, then work your way up to a fine grit.

7. Apply a finish to the spindle to protect the wood and enhance its appearance.

8. Repeat steps 4-7 for each additional spindle needed.

Spindles are an essential part of many woodworking projects, and designing and producing them requires careful planning and attention to detail. By following the steps outlined above and using the practical plan provided, you can create high-quality spindles that will add both functionality and aesthetics to your woodworking projects. Remember to choose the appropriate wood species, prepare the wood properly, use a lathe to shape the spindle, and sand and finish it to perfection. With patience and practice, you can master the art of spindle production and create beautiful and functional pieces for your woodworking projects.

Platters

Platters are wooden plates or dishes that can be used for serving food or as decorative pieces. They are popular woodworking projects because they are relatively simple to make and can be customized in a variety of ways. In this article, we will discuss how to design and produce platters, including the necessary tools, materials, and techniques.

Designing a Platter:

The first step in producing a platter is to design it. The design will depend on the intended use of the platter and the desired aesthetic. Some things to consider when designing a platter include:

a. Size: Determine the size of the platter based on its intended use. A larger platter may be suitable for serving a main course, while a smaller platter may be better for serving appetizers or desserts.

b. Shape: Consider the shape of the platter. Platters can be round, oval, rectangular, or any other shape. The shape will affect the functionality of the platter and its aesthetic appeal.

c. Wood Type: Choose a wood type that suits the design and intended use of the platter. Hardwoods such as maple, cherry, and walnut are popular choices for platters because they are durable and have a beautiful grain pattern.

d. Finish: Decide on the finish for the platter. A food-safe finish, such as mineral oil or beeswax, is necessary if the platter will be used for serving food. Other finishes, such as varnish or lacquer, can be used for decorative platters.

Producing a Platter:

Once the design has been finalized, it's time to start producing the platter. Here are the steps involved in producing a platter:

1. **Select and Prepare the Wood:** Choose a piece of wood that is suitable for the platter's design. It should be free of knots, cracks, and other defects. Cut the wood to the desired size and shape using a table saw, band saw, or jigsaw. Sand the wood to a smooth finish.

2. **Create the Platter Shape:** Use a router or chisels to create the platter's shape. If the platter is to have a flat bottom, use a router to cut a flat surface. If the platter is to have a curved bottom, use chisels to create the curved surface.

3. **Add Decorative Elements:** Use carving tools or a wood burner to add decorative elements to the platter. This could include a pattern or design around the edge of the platter or a personalized message or design in the center.

4. **Sand and Finish:** Sand the platter to a smooth finish, starting with a coarse grit sandpaper and progressing to a finer grit. Apply a food-safe finish, such as mineral oil or beeswax, if the platter will be used for serving food. Other finishes, such as varnish or lacquer, can be used for decorative platters.

Tools Needed:

- Table saw or band saw

- Router

- Chisels

- Sandpaper

- Carving tools or wood burner

- Food-safe finish

Materials Needed:

- Hardwood (maple, cherry, walnut, etc.)

- Sandpaper (coarse and fine grit)

- Mineral oil or beeswax (for food-safe finish)

- Varnish or lacquer (for decorative finish)

Practical Plan

Here is a practical plan for producing a simple round platter:

1. Select a piece of hardwood, such as maple or cherry, that is at least 1 inch thick and 12 inches in diameter.

2. Cut the wood to the desired diameter using a table saw or band saw.

3. Use a router to create a curved bottom on the platter.

4. Sand the platter to a smooth finish, starting with a coarse grit sandpaper and progressing to a finer grit.

5. Use a wood burner or carving tools to add decorative elements to the platter, such as a pattern or design around the edge.

6. Sand the platter again to smooth out any rough spots created during the decorative element process.

7. Apply a food-safe finish, such as mineral oil or beeswax, to the platter.

8. Let the finish dry completely before using the platter for serving food or as a decorative piece.

Variations on this plan could include changing the size or shape of the platter, adding more complex decorative elements, or using a different type of wood or finish. By following these steps and using the necessary tools and materials, you can create a beautiful and functional platter that is perfect for serving food or as a decorative piece.

CHAPTER 8

FINISHING TECHNIQUES

As already established in this book, woodworking is an ancient craft that has been around for centuries. It involves the creation of furniture, cabinets, and other items using wood as the primary material. While woodworking has evolved over the years, one aspect that remains crucial is the finishing technique.

Finishing is the process of applying a protective coat to the wood to enhance its appearance, durability, and resistance to wear and tear. A well-executed finishing technique can make a piece of furniture or cabinetry stand out and look beautiful for years to come. Here are some reasons why the finishing technique is essential in woodworking.

Protection against moisture and wear

Wood is a natural material that can be easily affected by moisture, temperature changes, and wear and tear. A proper finishing technique helps to protect the wood from these elements and extend its lifespan. For instance, applying a water-resistant coat to outdoor furniture can prevent water damage and rotting, while a UV-resistant coating can protect the wood from sun damage.

Improved appearance

Finishing can enhance the natural beauty of wood and give it a polished, sophisticated look. It also adds depth and richness to the wood's texture and color, making it more visually appealing. Different finishing techniques can achieve different effects, from a natural look to a glossy or matte finish.

Enhanced durability

The durability of a piece of woodwork is crucial, especially if it is meant for everyday use. A well-finished piece of furniture or cabinetry can withstand wear and tear and resist scratches, scuffs, and other forms of damage. The finishing also makes the woodwork easier to clean and maintain, thus increasing its longevity.

Improved value

Finishing can significantly increase the value of a piece of woodwork. A well-finished piece of furniture or cabinetry can fetch a higher price in the market, especially if it is of high quality and unique design. A well-executed finishing technique can make a piece of furniture look luxurious and elegant, thus appealing to potential buyers.

Ease of use

A properly finished piece of furniture or cabinetry is easy to use and maintain. For instance, a finished tabletop is less prone to water damage, staining, and other forms of damage, making it easier to clean and use. A finished cabinet is less likely to warp or crack, making it easier to open and close.

Finishing technique is an essential aspect of woodworking. It enhances the natural beauty of wood, improves its durability, and protects it from moisture and wear. A well-finished piece of furniture or cabinetry can fetch a higher price in the market and appeal to potential buyers. Woodworkers should take the time to choose the right finishing technique for their project and execute it with precision to achieve the desired results.

Types of Finishes

When it comes to woodworking, finishes are an important aspect of the craft. Finishing a woodworking project involves applying a layer of protective coating to the surface of the wood to enhance its appearance, increase its durability, and protect it from environmental factors such as moisture and sunlight. There are several types of finishes that woodworkers can use, each with its own unique properties and advantages.

1. Oil Finishes:

Oil finishes are some of the most popular finishes used by woodworkers. They are easy to apply and provide a natural, warm finish that enhances the wood's natural grain and texture. Oil finishes penetrate into the wood and provide protection from moisture and other environmental factors. There are different types of oil finishes available, including Tung oil, Linseed oil, Danish oil, and Teak oil, each with its own unique properties.

2. Shellac Finishes:

Shellac is a natural resin that is extracted from the secretions of the lac beetle. It is dissolved in alcohol to create a finish that dries quickly and provides a hard, durable surface. Shellac finishes are ideal for small projects or pieces that require a high gloss finish. They are also resistant to heat and moisture, making them suitable for use on kitchen and bathroom fixtures.

3. Varnish Finishes:

Varnish is a synthetic resin that is used to create a hard, protective finish on wood surfaces. It is available in both oil-based and water-based formulations and can be used to create a range of finishes, from satin to high gloss. Varnish finishes are highly durable and can withstand exposure to sunlight and heat, making them suitable for outdoor furniture.

4. Lacquer Finishes:

Lacquer finishes are made from nitrocellulose or acrylic resins that are dissolved in solvents such as alcohol or lacquer thinner. They dry quickly and provide a hard, durable finish that is resistant to water and chemicals. Lacquer finishes are ideal for use on musical instruments and other high-end woodworking projects.

5. Wax Finishes:

Wax finishes provide a soft, lustrous finish that enhances the natural beauty of the wood. They are easy to apply and provide a protective layer that is resistant to water and other environmental factors. Wax finishes are suitable for use on furniture and other decorative items.

6. Paint Finishes:

Paint finishes are used to create a solid, opaque layer of color on the surface of the wood. They are available in a wide range of colors and can be used to create a range of finishes, from matte to high gloss. Paint finishes are highly durable and can be used to create a range of decorative effects, such as distressed or weathered looks.

Selecting the right finish for your woodworking project is important for achieving the desired outcome. The type of finish you choose will depend on the look you want to achieve, the level of protection required, and the type of wood you are working with. Always follow the manufacturer's instructions when applying finishes to ensure a professional-looking result.

Staining

Staining is a common technique used in woodworking to enhance the appearance of wood. It involves applying a coloring agent, known as a stain, to the surface of the wood. The purpose of staining is to bring out the natural beauty of the wood grain, create a uniform color across the wood, and provide protection against damage from the environment.

There are many different types of stains available for woodworking, including oil-based stains, water-based stains, gel stains, and pigment stains. Each type of stain has its unique characteristics and properties, and the choice of stain will depend on the desired effect and the type of wood being used.

Oil-based stains are the most commonly used type of stain in woodworking. They are made by mixing a pigment with a mineral spirit or other type of oil, and they penetrate deep into the wood fibers, providing a long-lasting and durable finish. Oil-based stains are also very easy to apply, and they dry quickly, making them an excellent choice for a variety of woodworking projects.

Water-based stains are another popular choice in woodworking. They are made by mixing a pigment with water or a water-based solvent, and they offer several advantages over oil-based stains. For one, they are less toxic and more environmentally friendly than oil-based stains. Additionally, they dry more quickly than oil-based stains, and they do not emit as much odor.

Gel stains are another type of stain that is becoming increasingly popular in woodworking. They are thicker than traditional stains and can be applied more easily, making them an excellent choice for vertical surfaces or other difficult-to-reach areas. Gel stains are also very forgiving, allowing woodworkers to adjust the intensity of the color as needed.

Pigment stains are a type of stain that contains finely ground pigments suspended in a binder. They are excellent for creating a rich, vibrant color on wood, and they can be used to achieve a variety of different effects, including an antique or distressed look.

Regardless of the type of stain used, the process of staining is essentially the same. It begins with preparing the wood surface by sanding it down to a smooth finish.

Once the wood is smooth, it should be cleaned thoroughly to remove any dust or debris that may interfere with the staining process.

Next, the stain is applied to the wood using a brush or other applicator. It is important to apply the stain evenly and in the direction of the wood grain to ensure a uniform finish. After the stain has been applied, it should be allowed to dry completely before any additional coats are added.

If multiple coats of stain are desired, each coat should be allowed to dry completely before the next coat is applied. Once the final coat has been applied, the wood should be allowed to dry completely before any additional finishing products are added.

Always remember that staining is a crucial technique in woodworking that allows woodworkers to enhance the natural beauty of wood, create a uniform color, and provide protection against damage from the environment. By selecting the right type of stain and following the proper staining techniques, woodworkers can achieve a beautiful, long-lasting finish on their woodworking projects.

Varnishing

Varnishing is a common finishing technique used in woodworking to protect and enhance the appearance of wood. It involves applying a transparent or semi-transparent coating, typically made of a combination of resins, solvents, and drying oils, to the surface of wood.

The primary purpose of varnishing is to protect wood from moisture, scratches, and other forms of wear and tear. Varnish creates a hard, durable coating that prevents water and other liquids from penetrating the wood and causing damage. It also helps to prevent scratches and other forms of physical damage, which can mar the appearance of wood over time.

In addition to protecting wood, varnishing can also enhance its appearance. Varnish can bring out the natural beauty of wood by accentuating the grain and color of the wood. Some varnishes contain tinted pigments that can change the color of the wood or enhance its natural hue.

There are many different types of varnish available, each with its own unique properties and uses. The most common types of varnish include polyurethane, shellac, lacquer, and oil-based varnishes. Each type of varnish has its own strengths and weaknesses, so it is important to choose the right varnish for the job.

Polyurethane varnish is a popular choice for woodworkers because it is durable and easy to apply. It forms a tough, clear coating that is resistant to moisture, heat, and chemicals. Polyurethane varnish can be applied with a brush, spray gun, or roller, and it is available in both oil-based and water-based formulations.

Shellac is another popular varnish that is derived from the secretions of the lac beetle. It is available in both clear and tinted formulations, and it is typically applied with a brush or spray gun. Shellac is known for its quick-drying time and its ability to create a glossy, hard finish.

Lacquer is a fast-drying varnish that is often used on furniture and other wooden objects. It creates a durable, high-gloss finish that is resistant to scratches and other forms of wear and tear. Lacquer is typically applied with a spray gun, and it requires several coats to achieve a smooth, even finish.

Oil-based varnishes are made from a combination of natural oils, resins, and solvents. They are known for their durability and their ability to enhance the natural beauty of wood. Oil-based varnishes are typically applied with a brush or roller, and they require several coats to achieve a smooth, even finish.

When applying varnish to wood, it is important to follow a few key steps to ensure a smooth, even finish. First, the wood should be sanded and cleaned to remove any dirt, dust, or other debris. Next, the varnish should be applied in thin, even coats, with ample drying time between each coat. Finally, the varnish should be allowed to dry completely before the wood is sanded and buffed to a high shine.

Varnishing remains an important finishing technique used in woodworking to protect and enhance the appearance of wood. There are many different types of varnish available, each with its own unique properties and uses. By choosing the right varnish for the job and following the proper application techniques, you can create beautiful and durable finishes.

Polyurethane

Polyurethane is a versatile and widely-used synthetic material that has become an essential component in woodworking. It is a polymer that is created by combining diisocyanates and polyols through a chemical reaction. The resulting material is highly durable, flexible, and resistant to chemicals, abrasion, and impact. Polyurethane is used in woodworking for a variety of purposes, including as a protective finish for wooden surfaces.

There are two main types of polyurethane: water-based and oil-based. Water-based polyurethane is a popular choice for woodworking because it is low in odor and emits fewer volatile organic compounds (VOCs) than its oil-based counterpart. It dries faster, is less prone to yellowing, and is easier to clean up with soap and water. However, it is generally less durable and may require more coats to achieve the same level of protection as oil-based polyurethane.

Oil-based polyurethane, on the other hand, is known for its durability and resistance to wear and tear. It provides a rich, deep color to the wood and enhances its natural beauty. It is also highly resistant to water and chemicals, making it ideal for use in high-traffic areas or in areas that are exposed to moisture. However, it emits strong fumes and requires solvents such as mineral spirits or turpentine for cleanup.

Polyurethane is available in several forms, including spray, brush-on, and wipe-on. Spray polyurethane is typically used for large surfaces or for projects that require a quick and even application. Brush-on polyurethane is ideal for smaller areas or for projects that require more precise application. Wipe-on polyurethane is a thinner version of brush-on polyurethane that can be applied with a cloth or sponge.

Before applying polyurethane to a wooden surface, it is important to prepare the surface by sanding it to a smooth finish and removing any dust or debris. It is also important to ensure that the wood is dry and free from any oils or other contaminants. When applying polyurethane, it is recommended to work in a well-ventilated area and to wear protective gear such as gloves and a respirator.

Polyurethane is a popular choice for protecting and enhancing the natural beauty of wood. It provides a durable, long-lasting finish that is resistant to wear and tear, water, and chemicals. Whether you are a professional woodworker or a DIY enthusiast, polyurethane is a versatile and reliable option for all of your woodworking needs.

As we conclude this chapter, I want to emphasize that the various finishing techniques, as enumerated, are a vital aspect of woodworking. They protect the wood from damage while enhancing its natural beauty. By selecting the appropriate finishing technique for your project, you can ensure that your finished product will be both beautiful and durable.

Gabriel Andrews

CHAPTER 9

ADVANCED WOODWORKING PROJECTS

Advanced woodworking projects are those that require a higher degree of skill and experience than basic woodworking projects. They typically involve more intricate designs, specialized tools, and advanced techniques.

One of the most important things to keep in mind when embarking on an advanced woodworking project is to have a detailed plan in place before beginning. This includes everything from selecting the right wood for the project to designing the project itself and creating a detailed set of blueprints or plans.

Advanced woodworking projects may include complex joinery techniques such as mortise and tenon joints, dovetail joints, and finger joints. These joints require a high degree of accuracy and precision in order to create a strong and durable finished product.

Another common feature of advanced woodworking projects is the use of advanced tools and machinery. This might include specialized saws, planers, and routers, as well as advanced hand tools such as chisels and hand planes.

Examples of advanced woodworking projects might include building a hand-carved rocking chair, a wooden boat, or a intricately detailed piece of furniture such as a desk or bookcase. These types of projects require a high degree of skill and patience, as well as a deep understanding of the properties of wood and how it behaves under different conditions.

While advanced woodworking projects can be challenging, they can also be extremely rewarding for those who are passionate about woodworking. By taking the time to carefully plan and execute an advanced project, woodworkers can create truly unique and beautiful pieces that will be treasured for a long time.

Intarsia

Intarsia is a form of woodworking that involves the use of different types of wood to create intricate and detailed designs that can be used as decorative pieces or as functional items. This technique involves the use of a scroll saw or bandsaw to cut small pieces of wood, which are then fit together like a jigsaw puzzle to create a larger image. Intarsia can be used to create a wide variety of items, including furniture, wall hangings, and even jewelry boxes.

To get started with intarsia woodworking, you will need to gather a few basic tools and materials. These may include a scroll saw or bandsaw, various types of wood in different colors and grains, sandpaper, glue, and a pattern or design for your project. You will also need a good workspace with plenty of light and ventilation.

The first step in intarsia woodworking is to select the design for your project. There are many sources for intarsia patterns, including books, magazines, and online resources. Once you have your design, you will need to transfer it onto your wood using tracing paper or carbon paper. This will help you to cut out the individual pieces of wood more accurately.

Next, you will need to cut out the individual pieces of wood using your scroll saw or bandsaw. This can be a bit tricky, as you will need to make sure that each piece is cut to the correct size and shape. You may also need to make adjustments as you go along to ensure that everything fits together correctly.

Once you have all of your pieces cut out, it's time to start assembling them. This is where the real artistry comes in, as you will need to fit each piece together like a puzzle. You may need to sand down some pieces or make small adjustments to ensure that everything fits together perfectly.

Having assembled your intarsia piece, you can add any finishing touches that you like. This might include sanding down any rough edges or applying a coat of varnish or other protective finish. You may also want to add hardware, such as hooks or hangers, if you plan to use your intarsia piece as a wall hanging.

Overall, intarsia woodworking can be a challenging but rewarding project for advanced woodworkers. It requires a steady hand, a good eye for detail, and a lot of patience, but the end result can be truly stunning. With practice, you can create a wide range of intarsia pieces that are sure to impress.

Marquetry

Marquetry is a woodworking technique that involves the creation of intricate patterns or designs using small, carefully cut pieces of wood veneer. These veneers are arranged in a particular way to form a picture or pattern, which is then glued onto a substrate such as furniture, cabinets, or decorative objects.

The history of marquetry can be traced back to ancient Egyptian times, where it was used to decorate furniture and sarcophagi. It was also popular during the Renaissance in Italy, where it was used to create elaborate decorative panels and furniture.

The process of marquetry begins with the selection of the wood veneer. Different types of wood are used to create a variety of colors and patterns, and the grain of the wood is carefully considered to ensure that it matches the overall design. The veneers are then cut into thin strips or shapes using a scroll saw or a marquetry knife.

Once the veneers have been cut, they are arranged in a particular pattern or design on a flat surface, such as a workbench. The pieces are then glued together using a specialized adhesive that is designed to bond the thin pieces of wood together without adding excess moisture, which can cause warping or cracking.

After the pieces have been glued together, they are carefully sanded to create a smooth surface. The pattern is then transferred onto the substrate using tracing paper or a template. The marquetry pieces are then cut to fit the design and carefully glued onto the substrate, piece by piece.

Upon completing the marquetry, the surface is sanded again to ensure that the pieces are flush with the substrate. The piece can then be finished with a variety of coatings, such as varnish or lacquer, to protect the surface and bring out the natural beauty of the wood.

One of the key benefits of marquetry is its ability to create intricate and detailed patterns and designs that would be difficult or impossible to achieve using other woodworking techniques. Marquetry is also a great way to add visual interest to furniture or decorative objects, as well as to showcase the natural beauty of different types of wood.

In addition to furniture and decorative objects, marquetry can also be used to create art pieces such as wall hangings, picture frames, and even jewelry boxes. It can be used in combination with other woodworking techniques such as inlay or carving to create truly unique and beautiful pieces.

However, marquetry is also a challenging woodworking technique that requires a high level of skill and precision. It can be time-consuming and require a great deal of patience and attention to detail. The process of cutting and fitting the small pieces of wood together can be particularly challenging, as even the slightest mistake can ruin the entire piece.

This technique that has a long history and is still widely used today. It requires a high level of skill and precision, but can be used to create intricate and beautiful patterns and designs that are truly unique. Whether you are a professional woodworker or an amateur hobbyist, marquetry is a rewarding and challenging technique that can produce stunning results.

Scrollsaw Projects

Scrollsaw projects are a popular and challenging aspect of advanced woodworking. Scrollsaws are tools that are used to make intricate cuts in wood, plastic, and other materials. These cuts can be used to create decorative designs, patterns, and shapes, which can be incorporated into a wide range of woodworking projects.

To start with, it is important to have the right equipment. A scrollsaw is a power tool that can be found in most woodworking shops. It is a small saw that uses a fine blade that moves up and down rapidly to make precise cuts. The blade is attached to an arm that is suspended above a flat work surface. The saw can be adjusted to make angled cuts or to cut different depths into the material being worked on.

One of the most popular scrollsaw projects is making wooden puzzles. These puzzles can be made in a variety of shapes and sizes and can be challenging to complete. To make a wooden puzzle, the first step is to choose a design. Many patterns are available online, or you can create your own. Once you have the design, you will need to transfer it to the wood using a carbon paper or tracing paper. After that, you can use the scrollsaw to cut out the pieces of the puzzle. The pieces will need to fit together perfectly, so it is important to make precise cuts.

Another popular scrollsaw project is making wooden toys. Wooden toys can be simple or complex, and they can be made in a variety of shapes and sizes. One of the benefits of making wooden toys is that they are durable and can be passed down from generation to generation. To make a wooden toy, you will need to choose a design and transfer it to the wood. Then, you can use the scrollsaw to cut out the pieces of the toy. The pieces will need to fit together snugly, so it is important to make precise cuts.

Scrollsaw projects can also be used to create intricate wooden decorations, such as plaques, signs, and ornaments. These items can be used to decorate a home or office and can be personalized with names or special dates. To make a wooden decoration, you will need to choose a design and transfer it to the wood. Then, you can use the scrollsaw to cut out the design. Once the design is cut out, you can sand it smooth and apply a finish to protect the wood.

In addition to these projects, scrollsawing can also be used to create intricate patterns in wood, which can be used to decorate furniture or other woodworking projects. For example, you can use a scrollsaw to cut out a design in the top of a wooden box, or to create a pattern on the legs of a table. These patterns can be simple or complex, depending on your skill level and the design you choose.

Finally, scrollsaw tasks are both difficult and rewarding aspects of advanced woodworking. They take time, accuracy, and attention to detail, but the results can be breathtaking. Scrollsawing is a skill that can be utilized to improve a broad range of woodworking products, whether you are building puzzles, toys, decorations, or patterns. Therefore, if you're up for a challenge, try scrollsawing and see what you can come up with.

Carving

Carving is a woodworking technique that involves shaping and cutting wood to create intricate designs, patterns, and textures. It is a skilled craft that has been used for centuries to create ornate furniture, decorative objects, and architectural features. Carving can be done using a variety of tools, including chisels, knives, gouges, and saws, and can be executed on a wide range of wood types.

To begin a carving project, it is important to start with the right type of wood. Some of the most popular woods for carving include basswood, mahogany, cherry, and walnut. Each wood has its unique characteristics that affect the way it is carved, including its hardness, grain pattern, and texture.

Once you have chosen your wood, it's time to start carving. There are several different carving techniques that you can use, depending on the type of design you want to create. Here are some of the most common carving techniques used in woodworking:

1. **Relief Carving:** This technique involves carving away the background of a design, leaving the foreground design in relief. This technique is often used to create intricate designs on furniture, picture frames, and decorative objects.

2. **Incised Carving:** This technique involves cutting into the surface of the wood to create a design. It is often used to create fine lines and details, and is commonly seen on furniture and decorative objects.

3. **Chip Carving:** This technique involves using a knife to remove small chips of wood from the surface of the wood to create a design. This technique is often used to create geometric patterns and is commonly seen on boxes and other small decorative objects.

4. **Pierced Carving:** This technique involves cutting through the wood to create a design that allows light to pass through. This technique is often used to create decorative panels for doors and windows.

5. **Carved Molding:** This technique involves carving intricate designs into the surface of a piece of wood molding. This technique is commonly used in architectural features such as doorways and fireplace mantels.

When carving, it is important to have the right tools for the job. Some of the most common carving tools include chisels, gouges, knives, and saws. Each tool is designed for a specific type of carving, and it is important to choose the right tool for the job to achieve the desired results.

Carving can be a time-consuming process that requires patience and attention to detail. It is important to work slowly and carefully, taking breaks when needed to avoid mistakes and fatigue. Before starting a carving project, it is a good idea to create a detailed sketch or plan of the design to help guide your carving.

Generally, carving is a skilled woodworking technique that can be used to create intricate designs, patterns, and textures on a wide range of wood types. Whether you are carving furniture, decorative objects, or architectural features, the right tools, techniques, and wood selection are crucial to achieving the desired results. With practice and patience, anyone can learn to carve and create beautiful, unique pieces of art.

Gabriel Andrews

CHAPTER 10

SAFETY CONSIDERATIONS

Woodworking is a fascinating and rewarding hobby, but it also involves the use of sharp tools and heavy machinery, which can pose a significant risk of injury if proper safety measures are not taken. As such, it is essential to understand the safety considerations associated with woodworking before starting any project.

The first and most crucial consideration is personal protective equipment (PPE). PPE includes items such as safety glasses, hearing protection, dust masks or respirators, and gloves. It is essential to wear appropriate PPE at all times when working with wood, as it helps to protect against injuries and hazards such as dust, splinters, and noise.

Another important safety consideration is the proper use and maintenance of tools and equipment. Always use tools according to the manufacturer's instructions, and make sure they are in good working order before use. Regular maintenance and inspection of tools and equipment are also essential to ensure they are in good condition and safe to use.

Workshop safety is another critical consideration. A workshop should be well-lit and well-ventilated, with a clear and clutter-free workspace. Make sure all tools and equipment are properly stored and secured when not in use, and ensure that all power cords are in good condition and not damaged.

It is also important to have a first-aid kit readily available in the workshop, as well as a phone or other means of communication in case of emergency. It is also advisable to have a fire extinguisher on hand, and to know how to use it in case of a fire.

As a woodworker, it is crucial to always be mindful of your surroundings and the people around you when working with wood. Never rush a project, and take breaks as needed to avoid fatigue and reduce the risk of accidents.

The art of woodworking can be a safe and enjoyable profession or hobby, provided that proper safety measures are taken. By wearing appropriate PPE, properly maintaining tools and equipment, maintaining a safe and clutter-free workspace, having a first-aid kit and emergency communication available, and being mindful of your surroundings, you can minimize the risks associated with woodworking and enjoy your projects with confidence.

General Safety Guidelines

Woodworking is an enjoyable and fulfilling hobby that can result in beautiful pieces of furniture or art. However, it is also an activity that involves sharp tools and potentially dangerous equipment. Therefore, it is essential to follow general safety guidelines to avoid accidents and injuries.

Wear Proper Safety Gear

When working with wood, you should always wear the appropriate safety gear. This includes safety glasses to protect your eyes from sawdust and other debris, earplugs or earmuffs to protect your ears from loud noise, and a dust mask to prevent inhaling sawdust. Additionally, you should wear clothing that fits closely to your body, with no loose or dangling parts that can get caught in machinery.

Keep Your Workspace Clean and Organized

A clean and organized workspace is a safe workspace. Keep your workspace free of clutter and debris that can cause tripping hazards. Always put your tools and equipment back in their proper place after use. Additionally, make sure that your workspace is well-lit so that you can see what you are doing.

Familiarize Yourself with Your Tools

Before using any tool, make sure you are familiar with its proper operation and safety features. Read the user manual or watch instructional videos online to understand how to use the tool correctly. Never attempt to use a tool that you are not trained or authorized to use.

Check Your Tools Regularly

It is important to regularly check your tools to ensure they are in good working condition. Check for any loose or missing parts, frayed cords, or other signs of wear and tear. If you notice any issues, do not use the tool until it is repaired or replaced.

Use Proper Technique

Using proper technique when working with wood is critical for avoiding injuries. Make sure you use the right grip and stance for each tool and operation. Always keep your hands and fingers away from the cutting edge of a tool. Also, never use excessive force when operating a tool, as this can cause the tool to kick back and injure you.

Avoid Distractions

When working with wood, it is essential to focus on the task at hand. Avoid distractions such as using your phone or listening to music that may take your attention away from your work. Additionally, never operate machinery while under the influence of drugs or alcohol.

Be Mindful of Others

If you are working in a shared space, be mindful of others around you. Never leave tools or materials lying around that could cause someone else to trip or injure themselves. Additionally, be respectful of others' space and work, and do not distract them while they are operating machinery.

Have a First Aid Kit On Hand

Even when following proper safety guidelines accidents can still occur. Therefore, it is essential to have a well-stocked first aid kit on hand in case of injuries. Make sure the kit includes bandages, gauze, antiseptic, and other basic supplies. Additionally, keep a phone nearby to call for help in case of an emergency.

Practice Patience

Woodworking requires patience and attention to detail. Rushing through a project can lead to mistakes and injuries. Therefore, take your time when working with wood, and do not try to rush through a project to finish quickly. Additionally, take breaks as needed to avoid fatigue and maintain focus.

Attend Safety Training and Workshops

Finally, attending safety training and workshops is an excellent way to learn more about proper woodworking safety techniques. Many woodworking stores and community centers offer classes and workshops on woodworking safety and technique. Additionally, online resources such as videos and forums can also be a useful source of information and support.

In woodworking, it is essential to follow general safety guidelines to avoid accidents and injuries. Always prioritize safety when working with wood by wearing proper safety gear, keeping your workspace clean and organized, familiarizing yourself with your tools, checking them regularly, using proper technique, avoiding distractions, being mindful of others, having a first aid kit on hand, practicing patience, and attending safety training and workshops. By following these guidelines, you can enjoy woodworking while minimizing the risk of injury or accidents. Remember, safety should always be your top priority when working with wood.

Working with Power Tools

When working with power tools in a woodworking project, safety should always be a top priority. Power tools can be dangerous if not used properly, and it is important to take the necessary precautions to prevent injury. In this article, we will cover some important safety considerations to keep in mind when working with power tools in a woodworking project.

Wear Appropriate Safety Gear

One of the most important safety considerations when working with power tools is to wear appropriate safety gear. This includes eye and ear protection, gloves, and a dust mask. Eye protection is particularly important when using power tools that create dust or debris, such as a table saw or router. Ear protection is also important when using loud power tools, such as a circular saw or reciprocating saw.

Read the Manual

Before using any power tool, it is important to read the manual carefully. This will give you important information on how to use the tool properly and safely. The manual will also provide information on any specific safety precautions you need to take when using the tool.

Inspect the Tool

Before using a power tool, it is important to inspect it for any damage or defects. Check the power cord for any cuts or frayed wires, and make sure the tool is properly grounded. Inspect the blades or bits for any damage or wear, and make sure they are properly secured.

Use the Right Tool for the Job

Make sure you are using the right tool for the job. Using the wrong tool can not only lead to poor results, but it can also be dangerous. For example, using a circular saw to cut a piece of wood that is too thick can cause the saw to bind and kick back, which can be dangerous.

Keep Your Work Area Clean and Organized

A clean and organized work area can help prevent accidents when using power tools. Make sure your work area is free of clutter, and keep tools and materials organized. This will not only make it easier to work, but it can also prevent tripping hazards and other accidents.

Use Clamps and Other Safety Aids

When using power tools, it is important to use clamps and other safety aids to keep your hands and fingers away from the blades or bits. Use clamps to hold the material securely, and use a push stick or block to guide the material through the saw.

Keep Your Hands and Fingers Away from Blades and Bits

Never place your hands or fingers near blades or bits while the tool is in operation. Always use safety aids to guide the material through the tool, and keep your hands and fingers at a safe distance.

Turn off the Tool When Not in Use

When you are not actively using a power tool, it is important to turn it off and unplug it. This can prevent accidental starts and keep you and others safe.

Keep Children and Pets Away

Always keep children and pets away from your work area when using power tools. Even when the tool is not in use, it can be dangerous if a child or pet accidentally turns it on.

Bear in mind that working with power tools can be dangerous if not done properly. By taking the necessary safety precautions, you can ensure that your woodworking project is not only successful, but safe as well. Always wear appropriate safety gear, read the manual, inspect the tool, use the right tool for the job, keep your work area clean and organized, use clamps and other safety aids, keep your hands and fingers away from blades and bits, turn off the tool when not in use, and keep children and pets away.

Working with Hand Tools

Woodworking with hand tools is a rewarding activity that requires focus, skill, and patience. While power tools can speed up the process, many woodworkers prefer the control and tactile feedback that hand tools provide. However, as with any woodworking project, safety considerations are critical when working with hand tools.

Wear Proper Personal Protective Equipment (PPE)

The first step in staying safe when working with hand tools is to wear the proper PPE. Eye and ear protection are essential, as flying wood chips and loud noises can cause significant harm. Gloves can provide a better grip, but they can also increase the risk of injury, as they may get caught in machinery or blades. Therefore, it's crucial to wear the right type of gloves that fit well and don't get in the way.

Use Sharp Tools

Dull tools are more likely to slip or cause injury, as they require more force to use. Therefore, it's essential to keep hand tools sharp and in good condition. Use a sharpening stone or other sharpening tools to maintain the edge of your tools.

Handle Tools with Care

When using hand tools, it's essential to handle them with care. Never throw, drop or hit tools, as this can damage them and cause them to break or become dangerous. When not in use, keep hand tools in a designated area, away from other people and children.

Secure the Workpiece

When working with hand tools, it's essential to secure the workpiece to prevent it from slipping or moving. Clamps or vises can hold the workpiece in place, allowing you to work safely and accurately. Make sure that the workpiece is secure before beginning any cutting or shaping.

Use the Right Tool for the Job

Each hand tool has its specific purpose, and using the wrong tool can be dangerous and ineffective. Make sure that you have the right tool for the job before beginning any woodworking project. Use a saw for cutting, a chisel for shaping, and a plane for smoothing.

Maintain a Safe Work Area

Maintain a safe work area by keeping it clean and organized. Keep the area free of clutter and debris, and make sure that there is enough space to work comfortably. Use sawdust collection systems to minimize the amount of dust in the air.

Focus on the Task at Hand

When working with hand tools, it's essential to focus on the task at hand. Distractions can cause you to lose focus and make mistakes. Take breaks if you feel tired or distracted, and always keep your attention on the work.

Get Proper Training

Finally, if you're new to woodworking or unsure about how to use a particular hand tool, seek proper training. Many woodworking stores offer classes and workshops on using hand tools safely and effectively. These classes can teach you the proper techniques for using hand tools and help you avoid injury.

Working with Chemicals

Working with chemicals is an important part of any woodworking project. From glues to finishes and solvents, chemicals are used in nearly every aspect of the craft. Safety is a paramount concern when working with any chemical, and it's important to be aware of the risks associated with them.

First and foremost, always read the product's label and safety instructions before starting to work with any chemical. This is the best way to ensure that you're using the chemical safely. Take the time to understand the risks associated with the chemical and any protective equipment that's necessary.

It's also important to wear the proper safety gear when working with any chemical. This includes safety glasses or goggles, gloves, and a respirator. Even if a chemical is labeled as non-toxic, it's still important to take the necessary precautions. This is especially true if you're using multiple chemicals in the same area.

When mixing chemicals, it's also important to take the necessary precautions. Wear the proper protective gear, and make sure the area is well-ventilated. The fumes from certain chemicals can be dangerous, and you don't want to risk breathing them in. Additionally, always add the chemicals to the water, not the other way around. This will help reduce the risk of an accident.

In storing chemicals, ensure you keep them in a cool, dry place, away from any sources of heat or open flames. It's also important to keep them away from any food or other materials that could be contaminated. Additionally, store them in their original containers and away from any children or pets.

As a precautionary measure, always dispose of any unused chemicals in a safe and responsible manner. Check with your local municipality to find out the proper way to dispose of any chemicals. Never dispose of chemicals in the garbage, as they can be dangerous if they come into contact with other materials.

When working with chemicals, safety should always be your top priority. Take the time to understand the risks associated with each chemical you're using, and always wear the proper safety gear. Follow the safety instructions on the product's label, and make sure to store and dispose of any unused chemicals in a safe and responsible manner.

Taking these steps can help ensure that you're working with chemicals safely and responsibly.

Conclusion

Woodworking is an incredibly satisfying and rewarding hobby that offers endless possibilities for creativity and self-expression. Whether you're an experienced woodworker or just starting out, the skills and techniques you'll learn can be applied to a wide range of projects, from furniture and outdoor structures to small decorative pieces and even art.

In this book, we've covered the basics of woodworking, including the tools and materials you'll need to get started, as well as the essential skills and techniques for measuring, cutting, shaping, and finishing your projects. We've also explored a variety of woodworking projects, from furniture to small decorative items, outdoor structures, and even woodturning projects.

One of the most important things to keep in mind as you embark on your woodworking journey is safety. We've dedicated a whole chapter to safety considerations, including general guidelines as well as specific tips for working with power tools, hand tools, and chemicals.

Ultimately, the key to success in woodworking is practice, patience, and a willingness to learn and experiment. Don't be afraid to make mistakes - they're an essential part of the learning process - and don't be discouraged if your first few projects don't turn out exactly as you'd hoped. With time and practice, you'll develop the skills and confidence you need to tackle more advanced projects and create beautiful, functional pieces that will last for years to come.

Above all, enjoy the process of woodworking. Whether you're working on a small project or a large one, take the time to appreciate the beauty of the wood and the satisfaction that comes from creating something with your own two hands. With the knowledge and skills you've gained from this book, you're well on your way to a lifelong love of woodworking.

Glossary

Adhesive - A substance used for gluing wood pieces together

Adze - A tool with a curved blade used for shaping wood

Angle gauge - A tool used for measuring and marking angles

Arbor - A shaft used to hold and rotate saw blades or other cutting tools

Auger - A tool used for drilling holes in wood

Awl - A pointed tool used for making small holes or marking wood

Backsaw - A saw with a stiffened edge used for precise cuts

Bead - A decorative groove or molding along the edge of a piece of wood

Bending - The process of making wood pliable by steaming or soaking it, allowing it to be shaped and bent

Box joint - A joint used for joining two pieces of wood at right angles, with interlocking fingers

Bandsaw - A saw with a continuous blade used for cutting curves and shapes

Bevel - The angle formed between two surfaces

Biscuit joiner - A tool used to join two pieces of wood using a wooden biscuit

Bradawl - A tool used for making small holes in wood

Burnishing - The process of smoothing and polishing wood using a burnishing tool or material

Chamfer - A beveled edge along the length of a piece of wood

Chip carving - A decorative carving technique that involves removing small chips of wood to create a pattern or design

Clapboard - A type of siding made from thin, overlapping wooden boards

Clear coat - A transparent coating used for protecting wood while preserving its natural appearance

Coping - The process of cutting a molding or trim to fit snugly against an irregular surface

Crotch wood - Wood that is harvested from the junction of two branches or the base of a tree, often prized for its unique figuring and grain pattern

Cabinet scraper - A tool used for smoothing wood surfaces

Carving knife - A knife used for carving wood

Chisel - A tool used for cutting and shaping wood

Clamps - Devices used to hold wood pieces together during glue-up or other operations

Compass - A tool used for drawing circles and arcs

Coping saw - A saw used for cutting curves and shapes in wood

Crosscut saw - A saw used for cutting wood across the grain

Crown molding - A decorative molding used for finishing the top edge of cabinets, walls, and ceilings

Dado - A groove cut across the grain of wood

Dovetail joint - A joint used for joining two pieces of wood at right angles, with interlocking pins and tails

Dowel - A cylindrical piece of wood used for joining two pieces of wood

Doweling jig - A tool used for drilling dowel holes in wood

Drill press - A machine used for drilling holes in wood

Dust collection system - A system used to collect dust and debris from woodworking machines

Edge jointing - The process of creating a straight, smooth edge on a board

End grain - The exposed ends of wood fibers, which have a unique and often attractive appearance

Face grain - The visible surface of wood, which has a distinctive pattern and texture

Feather edge - A thin, tapered edge along the length of a piece of wood

Featherboard - A device used to hold wood pieces against a fence or table during cutting

Finger joint - A joint used for joining two pieces of wood end-to-end, with interlocking fingers

French polishing - A traditional wood finishing technique that involves applying multiple thin layers of shellac by hand

Forstner bit - A specialized drill bit used for drilling flat-bottomed holes

Gouge - A tool used for carving wood

Glue block - A small block of wood used to reinforce a joint or hold a piece of wood in place while gluing

Grease pencil - A waxy pencil used for marking wood that can be wiped away easily

Gouge - A chisel with a curved cutting edge used for shaping wood or creating decorative carvings

Grain direction - The orientation of wood fibers, which affects how it can be cut, shaped, and joined

Halving joint - A joint used for joining two pieces of wood at right angles, with half of each piece removed to create a flush surface

Hardwood - Wood from deciduous trees that is dense and durable, often used for furniture and flooring

Hand plane - A tool used for smoothing and shaping wood surfaces

Inlay - A decorative technique that involves embedding small pieces of wood or other materials into a larger piece of wood

Jigsaw - A saw with a reciprocating blade used for cutting curves and shapes

Jointer - A machine used for flattening and smoothing the faces and edges of boards

Janka hardness test - A measurement of a wood's resistance to indentation or wear, used to determine its suitability for flooring or other applications

Kerf - The width of a saw blade's cut, which affects the amount of wood removed during a cut

Laminating - The process of gluing multiple layers of wood together to create a thicker piece of wood

Lathe - A machine used for turning wood to create cylindrical shapes

Miter saw - A saw used for making precise angled cuts, typically at 45 or 90 degrees

Mortise and tenon joint - A joint used for joining two pieces of wood, with a square hole (mortise) in one piece and a corresponding projecting piece (tenon) in the other

Mallet - A hammer-like tool used for striking chisels and other woodworking tools

Mortise and tenon joint - A joint used for joining two pieces of wood at a right angle

Miter saw - A saw used for cutting wood at precise angles

Natural edge - The irregular, natural edge of a piece of wood, often left unfinished for decorative effect

Oil finish - A finish that penetrates into the wood to provide protection and enhance its natural appearance

Orbital sander - A sander that uses a circular motion to smooth wood surfaces

Panel saw - A saw used for cutting large sheets of wood

Particle board - A composite material made from wood chips and resin

Plane - A tool used for smoothing and shaping wood by removing thin shavings

Planer - A machine used for flattening and smoothing the faces and edges of boards

Pocket hole jig - A tool used for drilling angled holes for screws to join two pieces of wood

Rasps - Files with large teeth used for shaping wood

Router - A machine used for cutting decorative edges and shapes in wood

Relief carving - A carving technique that involves removing wood from a flat surface to create a raised design or pattern

Router - A power tool used for cutting decorative edges, grooves, or joints in wood

Sandpaper - An abrasive material used for smoothing and finishing wood surfaces

Sandpaper - A paper with abrasive particles used for smoothing wood surfaces

Saw blade - The cutting edge of a saw

Scroll saw - A saw used for cutting intricate shapes and designs in wood

Shellac - A type of finish made from a resin secreted by the lac bug

Spindle sander - A machine used for sanding curved surfaces and edges

Splitter - A device used to prevent kickback on a table saw by keeping the wood piece from closing in on the blade

Spokeshave - A hand tool used for shaping and smoothing curved surfaces of wood

Squaring - The process of ensuring that a board has 90-degree angles at all its corners

Stain - A coloring agent used to enhance the natural beauty of wood or alter its appearance

Table saw - A machine used for making precise cuts in wood with a circular blade

Tapering - The process of making a piece of wood thinner on one end

Tenon saw - A saw used for cutting tenons, which are projecting pieces of wood used for joints

Timber - Wood that is cut and processed for construction or other uses

Tung oil - A natural oil used for finishing wood that provides water resistance and durability

Varnish - A clear or colored coating applied to wood for protection and enhancement

Vice - A device used for holding wood pieces securely while working on them

Walnut - A hardwood with a dark, rich color that is often used for furniture and decorative pieces

Wax - A protective and decorative coating applied to wood surfaces

Wood filler - A putty-like substance used to fill gaps, holes, or cracks in wood

Workbench - A sturdy table used for woodworking operations

Made in the USA
Las Vegas, NV
01 October 2024

96102515R00125